MW01444849

I dedicate this book to ghost hunters
and paranormal investigators everywhere.

Paranormal Investigation

The Black Book of Scientific Ghost Hunting and How to Investigate Paranormal Phenomena©

Published by MajorVision International

2018

Artwork and design: **WWW.MAJORVISION.COM**

WWW.MAJORVISION.COM

Contents

Chapter 1: What is Paranormal, and What is Paranormal Investigation?

To many people, on face value, there is little or no difference between a paranormal investigator and a ghost hunter. This is not necessarily the truth. The word "paranormal" itself is formed by combining the word "para", which means above and beyond, and the word "normal", which means the currently explainable scientific world around us. Therefore, ghost hunting would technically fall as a category under the broader term of paranormal investigating.

Paranormal phenomena are defined as being beyond what traditional experience or science can currently explain. The way in which many paranormal phenomena are catalogued and explored is typically very different from how traditional science forms a hypothesis about a subject based on empirical evidence and then proceeds into laboratory-based experiments.

The subject of UFO's cryptozoology, ESP, telepathy, and extraterrestrial life all fall under the category of paranormal phenomena. To many, none of these things might sound very scientific things to study. Or are they? It's important to remember that there are some traditional scientists who believe in the paranormal. For example, the man who basically invented the modern computer and broke the German Enigma Code in World War 2, the amazing Alan Turing, was a firm believer in telepathy, which falls under the subject of "paranormal phenomena".

The possible existence of extraterrestrial life is not necessarily a paranormal subject any longer. This is because there are now many reputable scientists and scientific organisations which are actively engaged in the search for extraterrestrial life. Scientific-based projects such as SETI (Search for Extraterrestrial Intelligence) are conducting daily rigorous astronomical searches for evidence of intelligent life outside our solar system. However, in paranormal circles, the subject of the possible existence of extraterrestrial life mostly focusses on and around the UFO phenomena. In addition, there have been many aspects of the UFO phenomena which have occasionally suggested links to other apparently unrelated aspects of paranormal phenomena such as ghost hunting.

The cryptozoological aspect of paranormal phenomena is all about animals which are still unknown to modern science, or the continued existence of a species thought to be extinct. There have been numerous claims of cryptid sightings which have been well documented for centuries. There are probably several dozens, if not hundreds of different categories of cryptids that are claimed to exist globally. These include entities such as Bigfoot, Yeti, The Loch Ness Monster, Mothman, Vampires, Werewolves, Shape-Shifters, The Chupacabra, Dragons, Elementals, Demons, and The Jersey Devil, and so on.

Ghost hunting in the purest sense is primarily about the acceptance of and the investigation of the continuing existence of spirits which were once living human beings whose physical bodies are now dead. It also tends to merge into several other broader areas of paranormal phenomena, especially when studying elementals and similar entities.

Naturally, since ghost hunting also falls outside the purview of traditional science, all these things get broadly categorised under the term, paranormal. This is almost certainly why many modern ghost hunters commonly refer to themselves as being "paranormal investigators" and not specifically as “ghost hunters”. It’s also probably because it sounds better and more scientific.

The roots of modern ghost hunting can be traced back to the great era of spiritualism in the 19th and early 20th centuries. At the time, many organizations which were founded to investigate these phenomena, and some still exist today. Perhaps the best known of these classic organisations is The Society for Psychical Research. This organisation once boasted that it had as a member, the world-famous British author, investigator and creator of Sherlock Holmes, Sir Arthur Conan Doyle.

As well as investigating the spirits of deceased human beings, ghost hunters would typically become involved with the exploration of demons, angels, and human possession by unknown entities. Typically, these possession-based entities are almost always assumed to be a demon of some sort. The poltergeist phenomenon is also often investigated by ghost hunters. However, this subject almost certainly sits squarely between ghost hunting and the wider subject of paranormal investigation in general.

This is because there are certain aspects of the poltergeist phenomena which suggest that it might not be paranormal in nature. Instead, the ability to move objects could be caused by an individual possessing the ability to perform telekinesis. Telekinesis, or psychokinesis as it also called, is the ability to manipulate matter with the mind, and not through touch. It's also the ability to move objects through conscious or unconscious thought alone.

Technically, the concept of telekinesis directly violates several laws of physics. However, this hasn't stopped many governments around the world performing high-level scientific research into the subject. Apparently, there have been many people who once worked on such clandestine projects who have now made public what they were once witnessed. It seems that certain government departments in more than one country take the subject very seriously, while at the same time their PR teams make public ridicule of it. This transparent denial process only seems to fuel the belief and debate even further.

Unfortunately, many modern ghost hunters ignore a solid scientific approach, and instead, they rely on what I call techno-pseudoscience. The same has frequently been true in the past of many wider paranormal investigators researching the UFO phenomena and cryptozoological entities. This lack of scientific practice tends to place everyone who performs any sort of paranormal research and investigation under a degree of ridicule and disrepute. This includes the many paranormal investigators who only use a solid scientific approach in their research.

Many modern ghost hunting and paranormal TV shows typically only serve to severely damage the public image of paranormal investigation as a science. Many of these modern ratings-driven ghost hunting TV shows want you to believe that everything they encounter is a "dark entity", or a demon of some sort. Why not? After all, it seems that they have gathered large followings of people who don't really care and just love the drama of it all. Also, the better the ratings, the more money they make. The fact is that the majority of what you'll encounter during an average paranormal investigation is never usually an evil, dark entity.

Similarly, the TV shows which look for monsters and paranormal phenomena in dense forests have also done their part to damage the reputation of good paranormal investigators. Let's face it, there's nothing very professional or scientific about getting a group of armed obese rednecks to go out into the forest at night. Especially once they've boasted about their abilities like kids in a schoolyard, and then when they encounter a shadow or cracking twig they run for cover. Unfortunately, the most scientific thing you get to see as a viewer is a tree at night in a forest.

Is it any wonder why the traditional scientific community doesn't take any of this seriously? Where does this leave us, those genuinely interested in scientific paranormal investigation? Since traditional science currently categorically rejects, and often even ridicules the possibility of ghosts or other aspects of paranormal phenomena existing, it is very challenging when presenting scientific evidence. This is the point where I part company with mainstream science, even though I was trained in it for many years in my exercise science studies.

Since I was originally trained in the science of exercise and kinesiology, science will always be part of how I look at and analyse things. This includes all things paranormal. The more I became involved in paranormal studies, the more I began to wonder about how the laws of physics might apply to these phenomena. It is particularly fascinating to consider how certain aspects of quantum mechanics and uncertainty principles might be involved. Traditional science now supports the concept of our universe being part of a larger multiverse. This is a model of existence where many universes exist at the same time in conjunction with our own. In addition, science also now supports the concept that there are many other dimensions to our own universe, and for other universes too.

Everything in our universe is made of energy, and in one way or another everything is governed in some way by the laws of particle physics and quantum mechanics. The very particles that we're all made from have all existed as part of one form of matter or another for billions of years. Indeed, a large part of our physical matter was once literally stardust. This is because the oxygen, nitrogen, and carbon atoms that our bodies are made from were created in stars, just like our sun, over 4.5 billion years ago. Nothing is ever really destroyed, it only changes in form and is recycled to become part of another cosmic journey.

What if some part of our physical matter had a "memory" of everything we once were part of on that journey? Might this in some way affect us today? If it exists, then can this cosmic memory be accessed in some way by deliberate intention? Obviously, the questions that can be raised about this subject are almost endless. Furthermore, I'm convinced that in the future there will be many links and interconnections that we'll discover about quantum mechanics and certain aspects of what we currently call "paranormal".

One of the biggest problems that still persists is that we simply don't know for certain what the "spirit world" is, or where and how it exists. In many ways, it makes some sense that it might be another dimension that is running parallel to our own. In that dimension, they might be able to only "see" us over in our own dimension as shadow figures, in a similar way to which we can sometimes "see" them as shadow figures in their dimension. Maybe it's a little like we're each seeing the other through a pane of frosted security glass. Perhaps some sort of energy field or microvoid between the two dimensions causes everything to appear blurred and nebulous on the other side.

It could even be the case that each dimension of existence is part of a greater overall journey which we all must take. The famous paranormal author, psychic and broadcaster, Adrian Lee once hypothesised that even ghosts might be "die" in some way. He suggested that it seems from his own investigations that after a certain period of existence the "spirits" or "ghosts" seem to cease being able to contact our world. We don't know why this is, perhaps they simply ran out of energy. If Adrian is correct, then it's perfectly possible that they as "spirits" eventually move on to the next parallel dimension along on the greater cosmic journey. At that point they are then two dimensions removed from our plane of existence, making it impossible for them to communicate with us again. Perhaps this process of passing over into different dimensions goes on "ad infinitum" to coin the Latin phrase which means "to infinity" or "forevermore". Alternatively, it could have an end at some point, or in some way it may loop back around to the beginning for the circle to begin all over again. If it does, then this could at least partially explain the age-old beliefs that some religions have about reincarnation.

I believe that most, if not all phenomena that are currently considered to be paranormal in nature, will one day become part of accepted science. It is my belief that the phenomena that we currently consider to be paranormal, are simply beyond the knowledge of our current science. Let's not forget that we're still very much in our scientific infancy when it comes to observing, analysing and understanding these things. Perhaps mainstream science hasn't currently matured enough yet.

Mainstream science generally believes that we learn more through a progression of compound knowledge. However, this might not always be the case, especially when it comes to the realm of the paranormal phenomena. When it comes to studying these things, we may learn much more by also studying history and folklore from a serious forensic science perspective.

If you stand too close to anything, you'll never be able to fully see, understand, or completely comprehend, whatever it is that you're looking at. Instead, you'll always see only a small, distorted view. I believe that the same is true in all aspects of what is commonly called paranormal investigation. There's a much bigger picture to this subject, and mainstream science is all gung-ho about peering at it through a microscope and nothing else. If you try to understand a greater something by only focussing on a microscopic aspect of it, it will always mean that you're only seeing a very tiny piece of a much larger interconnected jigsaw puzzle.

I also believe that many aspects of what we consider to be paranormal, including extraterrestrial, are all somehow linked. This idea shouldn't be surprising. After all, there are many things which are paranormal in nature involving energy and matter manipulation at the atomic, and subatomic level. Demons, ghosts, and even extraterrestrial entities all seem to possess the ability to manipulate matter and energy to some degree. Perhaps extraterrestrials do this through the appliance of science which we currently cannot even comprehend. This is often clearly demonstrated in the extraordinary abilities which UFO's and some ET's seem to possess.

Mainstream science currently completely rejects the possibility of paranormal phenomena existing. This is primarily because the phenomena, and associated experiments surrounding them, cannot be repeated, proven and quantified by the classical methods of controlled multiple experimentations. I categorically reject these as being valid reasons. Mainstream science often conveniently forgets that there are several well-accepted fields of mainstream science that have similar issues in relation to repeated and controlled observational experimentation. Yet they are still all accepted as being solid and accepted science by those rooted in academia. The accepted scientific disciplines which don't conform to traditional methods of observational experimentation include astronomy, anthropology, and geology.

None of the aforementioned disciplines relies on the traditional repetition of experimentation and observation in controlled laboratory testing. If it's OK for these areas of science, then why should paranormal investigation be treated any differently? That's just pompous prejudice. There's nothing that could be less scientific than a scientist believing that they know everything and that there's only one way which is their way.

There have been countless times throughout history when revered scientists of the day have ridiculed the possibility of explanations that didn't conform with their current accepted science. If anyone had even suggested an explanation, which by chance was what we now know to be the correct scientific explanation, then they would have considered it to be either an impossible science or paranormal. I'm not even talking about anything very special or extraordinary. I'm thinking more about things which we take for granted every day such as, powered flight, road vehicles powered without the use of horses or other animals to move them, aeroplanes, space flight, lighting buildings without fire/torches/candles/lamps, humans diving for long periods under the oceans, etc.

The list of how the revered scientists of the day got it completely wrong is almost as endless as history itself. We don't even have to look very far back in history to see how accepted science and the scientists of the day would have laughed at the suggestion of things which we common knowledge today.

Of all the people who should by default have an open mind, mainstream scientists have always been the most closed-minded group of all. In this respect, they're almost as bad as the reformation puritan church, and the Vatican was, and perhaps still is. My point is, that just because we currently can't see it, taste it, hear it, smell it, touch it, or measure it, doesn't automatically mean that it doesn't exist. Instead, we just haven't developed our current science to the point where we can detect, measure and/or quantify it. It's that simple.

Furthermore, mainstream science now needs to get its head out of the sand where it's been buried for too long. It now needs to play "fast catch-up" with what governments and various religious leaders are now finally admitting about the UFO aspect of paranormal phenomena. Several governments around the world have now openly admitted that they acknowledge that there are aerial phenomena occurring within their airspace for which they have no current explanation.

How can they continue to deny it for much longer? Even the United States, has openly admitted to the existence of unexplained phenomena being seen and tracked. UFO's have been witnessed by reputable observers and tracked on both civilian and military radar all over the world. Astronaut Buzz Aldrin has even admitted to encountering UFOs during the first moon landing. UFOs have been chased by the fastest and most advanced aircraft in the world and our best planes appear to be primitive in comparison. Especially in how easy it is for UFO's to outrun and/or elude them while defying the laws of our current science as they do so.

When it comes to the wider subject of paranormal phenomena, it's clear that what we're allowed to believe, indeed "fed" to believe, is only the tip of a very large metaphoric iceberg. I'm completely convinced that there are agencies in certain governments in many of the developed countries of the world that know much more about other paranormal phenomena than they publicly admit. This includes the existence of ghosts, energy entities, spirits, interdimensional entities, UFO's, USO's, wormholes, and time travel.

Even Pope Francis and the Vatican have begun backing themselves "both ways" to use the racing analogy. If the existence of intelligent extraterrestrials becomes indisputable, they already have the PR teams ready with a plausible explanation. This is why there's been a gradual softening of church stance on the subject in recent years. Pope Francis even admitted that intelligent extraterrestrials could exist, and if they did exist then they would have also been created by "God". He even made traditional science appear ridiculously rigid in their thinking by saying in relation to the possibility of extraterrestrial life, "Until America was discovered we thought it didn't exist, and instead it existed."

Let's not forget that many world leaders have long been firm believers in the paranormal. Many of them have even had personal interactions with ghosts. Just after World War 2, Sir Winston Churchill was visiting the White

House in Washington DC. While staying there he documented that had an encounter with a full-body apparition, interacted with it, and gained a response. It seems that after taking a relaxing bath he walked naked into the bedroom where he came face-to-face with the ghost of Abraham Lincoln. In typical Churchill style, he recanted that he remained completely calm and said to the apparition, "Good evening, Mr President. You seem to have me at a disadvantage." The next instant, the apparition reacted to Churchill by smiling and then disappearing into the ether.

I mentioned earlier that the man who basically invented the modern computer, Alan Turning from Manchester, England, was a firm believer in telepathy. At the time, during the 1930s and '40s, this was considered by the scientific community as pure nonsense. Any "reputable" scientist of the day would have laughed at you if you'd have suggested that it was possible to read the thoughts and mind of another person. I'm sure that even Alan Turing was laughed at for his belief in telepathy by many of his peers at the time. Reputable scientists of the day certainly initially laughed at his ideas for building a computer, as did the military leaders. But where would we be without Alan Turing doing what they thought was impossible? He built the world's first computer and broke the so-called unbreakable Enigma Code at Bletchley Park during World War 2. This one action alone had a dramatic impact on the outcome of the war. Historians now estimate that the amazing Manchester-man, Alan Turing, made a breakthrough discovery that shortened the war by as much as 4 years, saving the lives of as many as 21 million people!

Fast-forward to today, 2018. Now we have scientists telling us that they have proof that all human brains are somehow interconnected together by what they describe as a low-level energy field. Professor Tatum, who is Sheffield University's Clinical Professor of Psychotherapy, said in a quote to the UK's Sunday Telegraph in January 2018, "We can know directly about other people's emotions and what they are paying attention to. It is based on the direct connection between our brains and other people's and between their brain and ours. I call this the interbrain."

This low-level energy field is basically a human interconnected internet, and it goes towards explaining how some people can seemingly read the mind of others. It also has an enormous impact on our current thinking about telepathy. This finding should also impact thinking and belief about the possibility of an Akashic Record existing, and how certain people who are able to access it either at will or subconsciously.

Similarly, another recent scientific breakthrough has had a direct effect on the belief about mind reading and telepathy. A new device that can literally read minds has been pioneered by the University of California and was recently reported in the Journal of Neural Engineering. The machine can translate what you're thinking and immediately display it as text on a computer screen with an accuracy rate of about 90%. It works by the machine registering and then analysing the combination of vowels and consonants used to construct a sentence in our mind. The computer then interprets the sentences based on the neural signals that are produced from thought alone and are then translated into real-time text.

Several companies are now producing mind-reading headsets that allow you to type silently on your computer through the power of what you're thinking. It works through sensors in the headset on several key points along the jaw and chin. These pick up the neural impulses produced by thought, and a computer then translates them into text. There are other companies that are going even further to develop complete computer-brain interfaces.

The fact is that for thousands of years, some people have clearly demonstrated the ability to predict future events in great detail, and/or read the minds of others with great accuracy. Up until recently, most people and especially those in the traditional scientific community had laughed at all of this as being unscientific nonsense. However, these new breakthrough discoveries have already changed much of the outdated thinking about these concepts. Now even the most traditional of scientists must force their mind to open-up enough to at least wonder and explore the blatantly obvious connections.

I was privileged to witness an amazing example of physic ability demonstrated by the leader of the Minnesota Paranormal Research Society (MPRS) in December 2014. I had always known that my good friend Heidi Steffens enjoyed an excellent reputation as a gifted psychic, but I had never witnessed a dramatic demonstration of her abilities until that time. She had travelled to Britain to meet me so that we could explore several potentially paranormally active locations for future team investigations. It was already mid-December, and since it was only two weeks before Christmas there were a lot of places to pack into our short week-long schedule.

I had planned out a workable itinerary which accounted for the heavier than normal pre-Christmas shopping traffic. At the end of the week, the day before she was due to fly back to the United States, I told her that we were going to visit an old friend. Since he was a great folk guitarist and singer, Stan Vannin had performed at The Hole in T'wall Pub in Bowness on Windermere without missing a Sunday performance spot for probably a couple of decades. The pub was built in 1612, and the name is a local contraction meaning "The Hole in the Wall". It was named that because the local smithy had a workshop attached to the pub. Legend has it that to save him time and to make life easier, he literally knocked a hole through the wall joining the two buildings so that he could be easily supplied with beer while he worked.

Since the pub was so old, I thought there might be a good chance that it was worthy of a paranormal investigation. When I told her about it, and that she'd also meet an old friend of mine, her expression changed. She then said to me, "Are you certain he'll be there?" to which I replied, "Of course he will, he's never missed a Sunday lunch gig there in years." She then simply replied, "OK then..." I didn't suspect there was any motive in her questioning me about it at the time, which was remiss of me. Even when she asked similar questions on several occasions during our week of travel, I still didn't think it strange. I was probably simply engrossed in maintaining the tight schedule we had to get through that week, so I wasn't as alert as I should have been.

Eventually, Sunday came around and the last day of our research dawned. We set out for Bowness on Windermere in the English Lake District early that morning. It was a typical grey, cold, overcast day with steely skies and a hint of frost on the ground. When we pulled off the motorway to head into the heart of the English Lakeland, an idea struck me. I suddenly remembered that there was another potential location not far out of our way which we could also explore. It was where a once famous person was born and lived there for a while. Without telling her that I was detouring, I changed course slightly and headed there instead.

This was Heidi's first visit there, so everything she had seen was completely new to her. She had absolutely no idea where we were, and no clue that I had thought of a bonus location to visit without telling her. We eventually arrived in the small South Lakeland town of Ulverston and parked the car at the side of the road in a very ordinary street. When I did so, she asked me if we were near the pub. I then told her that we were just taking a small diversion which wouldn't take very long. I then asked her to get out of the car, which she did, and to stand with her back to the house which we were parked beside. Again, she did exactly that. I then asked her to clear her mind and psychically link to the people who had once lived in the house behind her. I asked her to tell me all about the people who had once lived there.

She paused for a moment, closed her eyes and then began to speak. She told me that she could envision an old man who was obsessed with shoes and boots, she could also see a very young man who was equally obsessed but by something very different. This person she could "see" was obsessed by the world of the movies and movie making, but she added that the movies were a long way from where the house was. She then added that the young man had "rosy cheeks" when he was young and that he had a unique ability to make people laugh and feel like they were children again. After that, she could see no more.

I then told her that the house she was standing outside was number 3 Argyle Street, Ulverston. The house where world-famous comedian Stan Laurel of Laurel and Hardy fame was born and had lived before he moved to Hollywood to make an amazing 106 movies.

We then went to The Laurel and Hardy Museum in the old Roxy Cinema, in Brogden Street. The owner of the museum is always welcoming and generous to all guests, and he was more than happy to answer the questions I had for him. I asked him if Stan had always been slim, to which he replied, "No, he was quite a rosy-cheeked young man, look at this picture of him stood on the front step of the old house..." Thinking that Stan's parents had owned the house he was born in, I then asked him about them. We were then told that the house didn't belong to his parents, instead, it belonged to his grandfather. I then enquire about him. I was told that there wasn't much known about him, except that he was the local shoe and boot maker. Heidi had got every detail right about who had once lived in

3 Argyle Street, Ulverston. She had "seen" everything just as if she had been able to look back in time.

Still stunned from finding out all this, we then drove the comparatively short distance to The Hole in T'wall Pub in Bowness on Windermere. Once we'd parked the car and were walking towards the pub, she asked me once again if I was certain that Stan would be there. Again, I fleetingly dismissed any possible deeper meaning behind what she had said, and confidently told her that he'd be there. As we approached the pub I was suddenly struck by the absence of music and singing which would normally be filling the streets at that distance. Instead of hearing Stan's voice, there was nothing but silence.

When we went inside the curiously silent pub, we grabbed a drink at the bar and proceeded to go to the back room where Stan always sat while he played the guitar. The guitar was propped against a table, and there were drinks and cards on the table next to where he sat, but his chair was empty. I assumed that he'd taken a short break and I thought they were Christmas cards when I went over to read them. To my shock and horror, they weren't Christmas cards at all, instead, they were condolence cards. Stan had died that same week, on the very day that Heidi had landed in Britain and I knew nothing about it. Apparently, members of his friends and family had attempted to contact me. However, I'd changed my mobile phone number so the messages from them went unanswered.

I know for certain that Heidi could have known absolutely nothing about the plans that I changed at the very last moment on that day. She had never even visited the country before so it would have been impossible of her to simply recognise where she was from pictures in a guidebook. Besides, the house where she demonstrated her psychic powers was completely nondescript at the time. Therefore, the only way she could have sourced the detailed information when suddenly being asked to "tell all" was through psychic ability. She was somehow able to access the "human internet" as the scientists now call it, or perhaps even the Akashic records.

Whatever the answer might be, I just know that I was privileged to witness an amazing demonstration of the extraordinary psychic ability of Heidi Steffens. To date, this is one of the most impressive demonstrations of psychic ability that I have ever had the privilege to witness.

If you're already an experienced paranormal investigator, or you're about to become one, then this is a particularly exciting time. This is because never has there been more equipment to use, and well-known phenomena to investigate. Yes, at times you will still face ridicule and laughter from those with closed minds. Remember that a person closes their mind for many reasons. One of the most common reasons is because of their inability to cope with the bigger picture of the world, and our universe/multiverse being much bigger than they ever thought possible. In short, deep down they're simply scared of their place in the universe being redefined, and even their very existence is brought into question. It's all about deep-rooted their fear and insecurity.

Chapter 2: Scientific Ghost Hunting

To most people, the term “scientific ghost hunting” will sound like an oxymoron. However, this would be either an assumption or a conclusion to which they have automatically jumped to. No matter what your beliefs might be, there will always be a scientific approach which can be used to explore all phenomena. This includes ghost hunting and paranormal investigation.

Perhaps the first question one must ask would be, “What makes a process scientific?” A scientific process could be defined as being one which consists of systematic observation, the formulation, testing, and modification of hypotheses, together with experimentation and measurement. Scientific progress is made by using a process of checking conclusions against nature, and then after observing something, the scientist tries to explain what has been seen. The explanation of this is called a hypothesis, and there is always at least one or more alternative hypothesis. Scientific experiments are a procedure designed to test hypotheses. For a procedure to be termed “scientific”, a method of inquiry is commonly based on empirical or measurable evidence which is subject to specific principles of reasoning.

Therefore, if all prejudices are set aside, it is perfectly possible to approach ghost hunting and paranormal investigation in a scientific way.

Typically, ghost hunting is the process of investigating locations that are believed to be haunted. As a ghost hunter, you will also attempt to collect scientific evidence supporting the validity of the alleged haunting, and any other type of paranormal activity taking place at the location. In short, you'll be trying to find indisputable concrete evidence which will prove beyond doubt that ghosts exist.

The most important part of good ghost hunting is always going to be about maintaining a healthy and professional level of scepticism and objectivity. This is central to all good paranormal investigating. Simply "wanting" to believe at all costs, and by approaching things from an unscientific and unprofessional way, will only serve to undermine your overall objectives.

To help you maintain as high a professional standard as possible, I'd strongly advise you to only use the most rigorous of scientific methods in your approach. In fact, prior to beginning an investigation it's well worth performing extensive research into what would constitute a solid scientific approach. Since every investigation will be different, there will be some minor differences between each in this respect. However, the overall basic scientific model for each should be similar.

You should make every effort to eliminate and logically explain-away whatever evidence you encounter/gather/record. I dislike the commonly used term, "debunk". This is because it isn't very scientific to use slang vernacular when presenting serious evidence. Just imagine that you had captured the most compelling and indisputable scientifically derived evidence of the existence of ghosts, only to have your documented efforts undermined and mocked because of using slang terms. This would seriously call into question the validity of your supposed scientific methodology. Therefore, instead of using that term I use the term "eliminate", especially in any written or printed documents detailing the results of an investigation.

It's almost certain that any ghost hunt/paranormal investigation you'll undertake will not be performed under strict laboratory conditions. Therefore, you're almost never going to be able to perform the entire investigation as part of a completely sterile scientific plan. However, as part of the overall investigation process, you can identify specific parts which can be performed as a series of stand-alone scientific experiments. Sometimes you may only be able to perform one experiment during an investigation, while on other occasions it may lend itself to performing several. It will all depend upon the location, the control you have over it, your objectives, the equipment you have at your disposal, and the team you have in support.

To help you develop a basic framework for factoring-in scientific methodology into paranormal investigation I've outlined a simple plan. A similar process to this can be adapted and applied to all your paranormal investigations. This was the basic scientific process I was taught during my training as an exercise scientist while studying at university, and it is as follows:

1. Ask a pertinent question.
2. Perform background research.
3. Construct a hypothesis.
4. Test it in an experiment.

5. Ask, is the procedure working?
    a. If not, then revert to step 4 until the answer is yes.
    b. If yes already, then proceed below
6. Analyse the data and draw your conclusions.
7. The results are either in line with the hypothesis, or they're not.
    a. If the results are not in line with the hypothesis or are only partially in line, then the data gathered becomes part of your background research. From this, new questions can be asked. Go back to step 3 and form a new hypothesis, then perform the experiment process all over again.
    b. The results are already in line with the hypothesis, proceed below.
8. Since the results are already in line with the hypothesis, then publish, communicate, and present the results.

Naturally, the greater control one has over the location, then the greater the accuracy of the outcomes and conclusions which are drawn from it. I'll now explain the scientific critical-path process in more detail.

First, ask a question about something you believe that you will observe. Questions are all about, how, what, when, who, which, why, and/or where? This is the start of the scientific process. For example, "Will I be able to measure and record the dramatic temperature change that is reputed to happen at place X, in room Y, when a "ghost" or other paranormal entity is present?"

The second step is to perform solid background research about what you're investigating. Use whatever resources that are available to gather and collate the best data that has been recorded to date. This will also help you to work around any potential logistical issues, and to avoid mistakes that others might have made in previous experiments.

The third step, and often the most challenging part for most people, is the construction of an initial realistic hypothesis. Remember that a hypothesis is nothing more than an educated guess about how something might work. You're trying to answer your initial question with an explanation that can be tested by you in practice.

A well-constructed hypothesis will allow you to make some sort of a prediction about what you expect the outcome to be. For example, "**If** *this room is reputed to have a cold spot – then if you place a thermometer at position X –* (**this was you saying what you will do**) – *if the temperature changes when communicating with a ghost/entity/spirit etc.* - **then** - *it will be recordable and measurable during the encounter* – **(you're saying what will then happen)**

You should clearly state both your hypothesis and what you believe the resultant predicted outcome will be testing. Keep it simple, especially to begin with, and make your hypotheses, predictions and outcomes easy to measure and quantify. This will help you to begin incorporating the scientific process into more of your experimental research.

The fourth step is to then test your hypothesis by performing an experiment. This test is to see if your predicted outcome is accurate, or not. Make sure that you always perform a fair and valid test that can stand up to scrutiny. Record yourself, together with the processes you use every step of the way. If you need to change part of the experiment, then do so by changing only one factor at a time, with everything else remaining the same as you continue testing. It's a good idea to repeat the same experiment several times, with each test being properly recorded. This help to eliminate the possibility of your initial results being due to an accident.

The fifth step is to analyse the data you've gathered, and then draw a conclusion as a result. This is done by gathering all recorded measurements and then analysing them to see if they support your original hypothesis, or not. It's very common for scientists to find that what they predicted doesn't even come close to matching the outcome of their experiment. Therefore, don't be disheartened if this happens to you. It's more important to maintain good scientific practices during your investigative research.

If you got it wrong, then you've done nothing more than to find a way which doesn't work and can be eliminated from your list. Don't see it as a failure. Simply go back to the earlier stage and remodel your initial hypothesis, then start the process all over again. Once again, maintain your scientific methodology in your next experiment process.

If you get it right, then you can do one of two things. Firstly, you can decide if you want to run the same experiment again in a different way. If you get the same results, then this will only serve to strengthen the validity of the data/results you obtained. Alternatively, you may simply wish to communicate your results to others, together with the methodology and data that was gathered during your investigation.

Scientific Investigation and The UFO Phenomena

It's one thing to be able to use scientific processes to investigate paranormal phenomena in a semi-controlled environment such as a building or patch of land, but how can this process be applied to investigating UFO's? The answer is, typically, with great difficulty.

It's easy to allow our desire to believe in something to cloud our judgement and affect the quality of our investigative methods. "Wanting to believe" just isn't enough, there must be hard proof. Even though no one has found alien technology they can show off or a substantial section of an alien craft, it doesn't disprove their existence either. After all, the lack or absence of hard evidence isn't in and of itself evidence of the absence of aliens. Typically, all videos of UFO's are filmed from very far away. If a video merely shows unusual flashing lights, then what does this prove? It only proves that something has flashing lights such as a plane, helicopter, some other type of aircraft or even a UFO. We simply don't know.

It's clear that the key to solving the UFO mystery is by following scientific methodology when investigating the phenomena. The real problem lies with the nature of what is being investigated. This is something which "was" seen and/or filmed by somebody or several people. At best the UFO might be seen on both civil and military radar, and this is about the best and most scientific evidence that can be typically obtained. The problem is that no one ever knows when or where a UFO sighting will occur. This means that in attempting to investigate them, even the most scientific investigation processes are always after the fact when the UFO has long gone. With UFO incidents, all that investigators are typically left to work with are statements from eyewitnesses, and physical evidence left behind such as marks or burns on people, marks on the ground or scorched patches of grass. As far as visual evidence goes, they may have some blurry video or stills pictures, but usually not much more than that. Rarely, if ever, will they have any measurements, data or metrics of any sort.

My wife Helen and I were privileged to be involved in what is hailed by many professionals, including MUFON, as being one of the most significant UFO sightings of recent times. The reason for this is that the UFO incident happened in the middle of an outdoor paranormal investigation when we had already deployed a wide range of testing and measuring equipment which was already laid out and functioning when the UFO incident occurred. By sheer good luck, we were prepared in advance to take readings, measurements, and to gather metrics/data from a UFO incident. This is something that few others, if any, have been able to do previously.

The incident occurred on the 1st July 2017 in Redwood Falls, Minnesota, USA. During the previous week, my wife and I received a call from Adrian Lee, the paranormal author, psychic and broadcaster. He invited us to investigate with him and the leading members of his team at a highly unusual event. It was the 100th anniversary of the famous mass axe murder of 1917. This was when a man is alleged to have brutally murdered his wife and four children at their home. It was always believed that the husband was to blame, however, his innocence was strongly protested. Apparently, the real killer or killers somehow got away with it and slipped the net of the law at the time.

The Redwood Falls Museum curator, Patricia Lubeck, had kindly allowed the axe which had been used in the murder to be released for the evening. This was so that it could be used as a trigger object during the paranormal investigation. It is believed that a trigger object can often prompt a response from a ghost. The curator of the museum would accompany the axe to the Redwood Falls cemetery where the graves of the husband and the victims had been found.

We assembled at dusk on that Saturday evening and began the investigation at the grave of the husband. A comprehensive range of different types of testing and measuring equipment was laid out in a logical order. Every member of the team also held at least one additional piece of equipment. I held the axe that had been used in the murder which we hoped would be a trigger object to stimulate a response. Adrian led the way and began asking questions, and soon we were all asking questions according to the notes we'd prepared earlier. We were lucky because we received several answers and responses on certain pieces of equipment that appeared to be intelligent rather than random. We even got the names of two suspects who may have been the real perpetrators of the crime, and which might vindicate the husbands claim that he was innocent. From the historical data we read, it certainly seems that he was wrongly convicted on purely circumstantial evidence which would have been rejected evidence had the trial taken place today.

Feeling good about our achievements so far, we then relocated to the south side of the cemetery to the grave of the wife and children who had been murdered. Again, we went about setting up a whole range of equipment around the grave. This included a Mel Meter, magnetic compass, EMF detector, thermal imaging camera, night vision video camera, laser grid, Ovilus, static meters, motion detectors, and thermometer. Again, every team member each held a piece of equipment of their choice, and several of us had digital stills cameras as well.

The curator of the Redwood Falls Museum, Patricia Lubeck, then asked me which way magnetic south was so that she could reference it in her notes. I activated my portable GPS unit and attempted to take a reading. To my surprise it wasn't working correctly, in fact, I'd never seen it behave in the way it did with mixed up readings and a jumbled screen. I didn't think much about it at the time and powered it down as I picked up the magnetic compass. This is when things began to get strange because even this wasn't working correctly. It was a simple magnetic compass, the kind that you'd use when map reading while hiking. Therefore, there was nothing to go wrong with the unit because it was a simple needle and dial affair.

No matter what I did and which way I turned the compass, the needle had become locked on the "N" for North point. I rotated myself and the compass 360 degrees so that the North setting on the dial rotated with me, and the needle remained fixed on that letter without any deviation. It was exactly what you'd expect if you had a magnet held near the compass at that point. Again, since we were busy preparing equipment, I dismissed it and returned the compass to its pre-planned spot down near the gravestone. I then used natural navigation techniques to give Patricia the approximate position she had requested.

Since it was a clear and still night with excellent visibility and almost no wind, it wasn't difficult. The process involved me judging the time, the position of the moon, the location and orientation of the cemetery on the map I'd read earlier, and by observing the lines of commercial airliners I could clearly see about 10 miles South. This was where I knew the flight path into Minneapolis-St. Paul International Airport was. I've always been interested in aviation and some years earlier I'd received pilot training. Initially, this was in a 'Piper Warrior' with Ravenair at Manchester Airport in England which was a standard single engine prop-driven light aircraft. Later, I moved onto learning how to fly jet aircraft and received training in a Jet Provost with Zero-9 Squadron in East Anglia under Captain F. Harrigan.

With that small hiatus out of the way, we settled into what we thought would be the final phase of the investigation. Again, since this was Adrian's team he led the way by asking certain questions while I was stood next to him. Adrian was holding a ghost box, Heather Morris was holding a night vision video camera, Michelle Cory was holding a digital voice recorder, Helen Renee was holding a thermal camera, and Patricia Lubeck was holding a digital stills camera. Once again, I held the axe that had been used in the murder, the same one that had killed the people who were buried in the grave in front of me. Holding the axe at their grave was a little surreal, even for me.

At 2230 hours (10-30PM) Adrian had probably only asked two or three questions when my attention was caught by a light in the sky behind him. I then became completely distracted by it and had physically turned myself to look away from where we were investigating. I had never seen anything like this before, and I just knew that this strange light was not an aircraft. It was a large ball of flame-orange light with no aircraft navigation/ID lights, it was at a height of about 10,000 feet, about 2 miles away, and travelling at between about 3 to 400 miles per hour silently West to East on a horizontal trajectory.

I then interrupted the investigation and directed the team's attention to the unidentified light source. Everyone was stunned when the object suddenly stopped in mid-air, paused for about 10 seconds. It then vectored down about 30 degrees and then stopped for about 20 seconds. After that, it then resumed flying and headed off on an east-north-east trajectory until it disappeared in that direction.

We all instantly knew that we had suddenly become involved in what could only be described as a UFO incident.

Fortunately, apart from Patricia Lubeck, all the other team members present were highly experienced paranormal investigators. We'd trained ourselves in advance so that if we ever encountered and were suddenly faced with the "unknown", then we were all prepared to follow certain scientific procedures to log data. This way, instead of freezing on the spot or running away, we'd all remain calm and composed if we ever encountered something dramatic and unexpected during an investigation. However, when we originally devised the plan, we'd envisioned that we'd probably encounter something like a full-body apparition of a ghost. We never once thought that we'd be thrust into a major UFO incident.

This wasn't the end of it. Two more large balls of unidentified light followed the first one. The second was red, the last one was yellow, and each of them was precisely 5 minutes apart. Amazingly, they all followed exactly the same course and performed exactly the same manoeuvres and course changes at the same points.

The differentiating factor between this UFO encounter and almost all others is that we were prepared in advance with a wide range of testing and measuring equipment already deployed for another purpose. Therefore, we were immediately able to start recording and logging data about the entire incident without any delay. The advanced training we'd all put ourselves through as a team gave us the resources necessary to remain composed and calm so that instead of panicking, we all simply got on with the job of scientifically investigating paranormal phenomena, however, we encountered it.

All of the UFO's we encountered caused a significant spike in readings to take place on all our equipment, which is in line with what has been previously hypothesised but never actually verified and recorded. The representatives from Mutual UFO Network (MUFON) who interviewed each of us separately, said that this was probably one of the most significant UFO incidents of recent times. The following narrative is a transcript of the official report, together with some of the data that was recorded which we're allowed to make public now.

U.F.O. Incident Saturday, July 1st, 2017, Redwood Falls Minnesota, USA.

Redwood Falls Cemetery, Redwood County, MN, USA. The Redwood Falls Cemetery is in Redwood County. The county seat for Redwood County is in Redwood Falls.

GPS coordinates - Latitude: 44.5505° (44° 33' 1") Longitude: -95.0983° (-95° 5' 53")

People present:

1. Brian Sterling-Vete PhD: (BSV) British journalist, documentary filmmaker, author.
2. Adrian Lee PhD: (AL) author/historian/radio host/founder of The International Paranormal Society (TIPS), forensic historical researcher, an expert in semiotics.
3. Heather Morris: (HM) US government worker/radio host/member of TIPS and audio expert
4. Michelle Corey: (MC) US government worker/radio host
5. Helen Renee: (HR) author/designer
6. Patricia Lubeck: (PL) curator of the Redwood Falls Museum/author/historian

2 x Trained Observers On-Hand in the Team at the Time

Brian Sterling-Vete is a trained observer. He received pilot training in a Jet Provost trainer with Zero-9 Squadron UK under Captain F. Harrigan, and in Piper Warrior with Ravenair UK. He is a Search and Rescue Master Diving Instructor and trained by instructors from the Royal Marines Commandos in preparation for deployment into war zones and areas of civil unrest.

Adrian Lee is a trained observer. He is a forensic historian and expert in semiotics (the study of signs and symbols as a significant part of communications) of both the ancient and modern world. Working as a forensic historian and expert in semiotics it requires 1st class observational skills, together with the recording of data.

2200 hours, Comprehensive Range of Paranormal Detection Equipment Deployed.

The team deployed at the southern side of the cemetery.

They primed and deployed the following equipment for an experiment:

- EMF Melmeter
- 2 x K2 EMF meters
- I-Ovilus
- Ghost box radio scanner
- Compass
- GPS
- HD Video camera with night vision ability
- Digital Voice Recorder
- Static meter

- EMF radar

The problems which suddenly occurred:

- The compass became fixed on a locked trajectory, as if magnetised, despite turning it in all directions. We checked for stray/anomalous nearby magnetic sources, and there were none.
- The GPS also failed.
- Repeated attempts failed to get either device working again.
- The static meter measured a high reading.
- The ghost box radio frequency scanner behaved in a way that has never been known, emitting a strange undulating pulsing sound.

2230 hours.

BSV noticed a large bright flame-orange ball of light moving steadily on a horizontal flight path from east to west. He notified the group to its sudden appearance.

Estimated GPS coordinates of the east to west line of travel - Latitude: 44° 50' 50" - The approximate longitude when the object was first sighted: -95° 00' 00")

Please note from the MN flight map, no recognised flightpath exists for the approximate area where the object was sighted, and for the path it took.

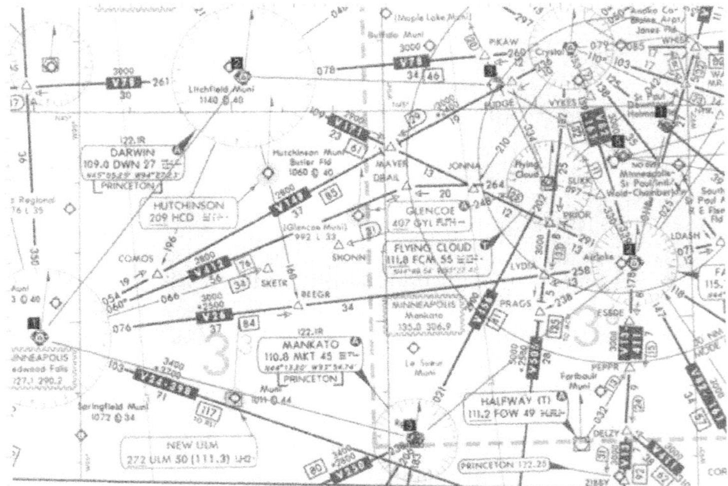

The EMF meters spiked and continued to spike while the object was visible into a reading of 25 milligauss.

The object was large, about 10,000 feet away, and travelling around 300-400 mph with no noise.

There were no aircraft ID marker beacons (strobes, red and green wing navigation/position lights etc.

The flight path to MSP airport was about ten miles south of us, behind where we were standing, and we could clearly see aircraft taking that path together with beacons.

The object dipped, and then stopped for about ten seconds, it then moved again and then stopped again for about twenty seconds before taking an east-north-east trajectory. It disappeared in that direction. We logged time and other data.

2235 Hours

Exactly the same occurrence then happened again, this time with a red ball of light.

All flight paths, trajectories, and movements/pauses were the same as if mirroring the first UFO. After the object disappeared, and when the time had been logged, Adrian then said that ***"it would be funny if another object appeared in another 5 minutes."*** So, we waited.

2240 hours

EXACTLY the same thing then happened again, in EXACTLY the same way, with a third UFO.

Once again, all flight paths, trajectories, and movements/pauses were the same as if mirroring the first and second UFO's.

The only difference was that this object was yellow, and the I-Ovilus produced the word "Yellow" at the same time as the sighting.

No other sightings were made. After each of the three encounters had finished, all equipment began functioning normally again.

Notes and Weather Data

The evening was calm, very little cloud cover, almost no wind, low-mid humidity, excellent visibility. The objects were moving much too fast to be a balloon or similar object caught in the wind. In addition, this, unlike the object, a balloon or similar would not and could not travel in a perfectly horizontal line, at a constant speed, emitting a steady ball of light, and then perform the manoeuvres which were observed. More importantly, two additional 'balloons' couldn't perform the same speed/height/direction/ manoeuvres while emitting light that way.

Redwood Falls, MN

Redwood Falls Municipal

4:16 PM CDT on July 17, 2017 (GMT -0500)

Weather History for KRWF - July, 2017

July

1

2017

View

Saturday, July 1, 2017

Daily Weekly Monthly Custom

	Actual	Average	Record
Temperature			
Mean Temperature	67 °F	-	
Max Temperature	82 °F	84 °F	99 °F (1974)
Min Temperature	63 °F	61 °F	46 °F (1969)
Cooling Degree Days	2		
Growing Degree Days	17 (Base 50)		

	Actual	Average	Record
Moisture			
Dew Point	60 °F		
Average Humidity	56		
Maximum Humidity	83		
Minimum Humidity	31		
Precipitation			
Precipitation	0.00 in	-	- ()
Sea Level Pressure			
Sea Level Pressure	29.84 in		
Wind			
Wind Speed	9 mph (West)		
Max Wind Speed	16 mph		
Max Gust Speed	17 mph		
Visibility	10 miles		

Daily Weather History Graph

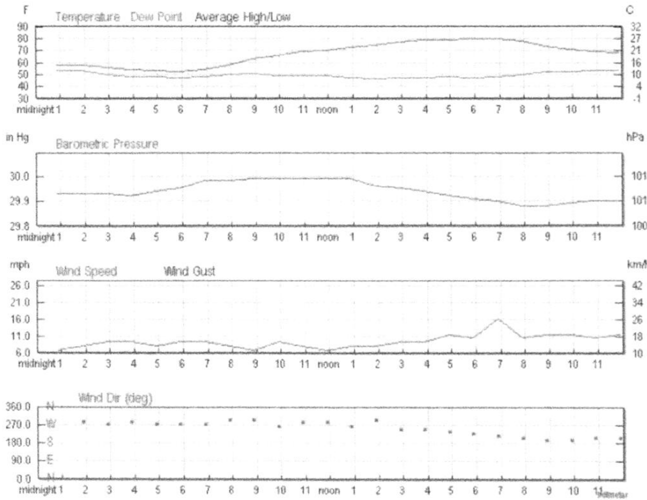

Here is a sequence of still pictures taken from the night vision video cameras we had with us at the time. The sequence shows how I initially spotted the UFO, and then how Adrian and the rest of the team were alerted.

This shot shows me on the left, and Adrian on the right, as the investigation has just begun.

This shot shows me on the left as I spot the first UFO

This sequence of screen grab stills was captured by one of the night vision video cameras.

In order from top to bottom. The top screen grab is the first UFO which was orange.

The second screen grab in middle is the second UFO which was red.

The third and last screen grab at the bottom is the last UFO which was yellow.

The word "yellow" popped up on the Ovilus when it appeared.

At the time of writing this book, the incident is still under official investigation, so not much more can be said about it at this time. What I can tell you was that once the incident was over, and we'd all re-composed ourselves, then we discovered the real effect it had on us. We were all considerably shaken by what we'd encountered together with the data we'd recorded to substantiate it.

After the cemetery part of the investigation was complete we then went to the Redwood Falls Museum as planned. We continued to investigate the old jailhouse which is at the rear of the building where the condemned husband in the axe murder case of 1917 spent his last night before the execution. Once again, our advanced training to follow scientific methods of investigation paid off. Since we were all still in a certain degree of shock from the UFO incident, thanks to our training we continued to document some excellent evidence of paranormal activity.

I cannot stress strongly enough that it is vital for all team members to undergo advanced preparation and systematic training. The training should attempt to emulate the most stressful and challenging conditions that might be experienced during any paranormal investigation. Furthermore, the training should be repeated on a regular basis so that it becomes second nature for all team, members. This is the only way to help ensure success if or when you and your team is suddenly faced with a stressful, challenging, and possibly unnerving situation. This way they'll not only follow the proper safety procedures, but they'll stick to their training in following scientific data collecting methods to gather the best evidence supported by as much data as possible about the phenomena.

Now that you are more conversant with what constitutes a scientific approach to ghost hunting and other kinds of paranormal investigation. You're now ready to move on to the next step. In various sections of the book, according to where it best fits, I'll offer some tips and ideas about what sort of advanced training you might want to include for you and your team.

Now you'll need to identify something that is worthy of investigation. This will typically be a building of some sort, but an outdoor location would be perfectly acceptable too. Once you have done this, you'll then need to draw up an outline of a plan of how you will perform the investigation. This should include any specific controlled scientific tests that you will perform as part of it.

You'll also need to draw up an equipment list based on an ideal scenario with everything you need at your disposal. This should include the equipment that you already have, equipment that other team members could bring with them, as well as the ideal team of people that will be needed to complete a successful investigation.

NOTE: On the next page is a recap in visual flowchart format of the scientific procedure process which can be applied to many of your investigations. The page can be photocopied to help train all team members to follow the same scientific critical pathways. A copy may also be useful when on location while setting up for an investigation.

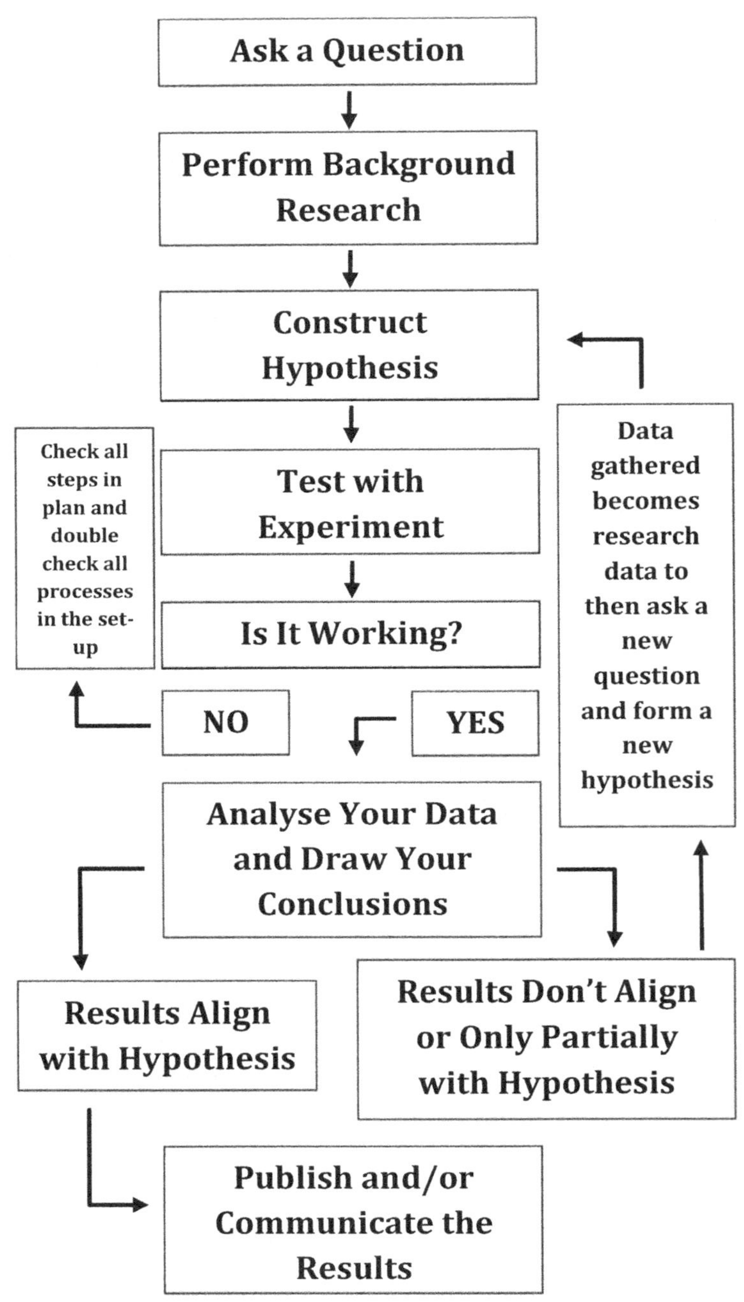
Ask a Question
Perform Background Research
Construct Hypothesis
Test with Experiment
Is It Working?
Check all steps in plan and double check all processes in the set-up
NO
YES
Data gathered becomes research data to then ask a new question and form a new hypothesis
Analyse Your Data and Draw Your Conclusions
Results Align with Hypothesis
Results Don't Align or Only Partially with Hypothesis
Publish and/or Communicate the Results

Chapter 3: Paranormal Terminology

As a paranormal investigator, you'll get to hear many unusual terms, phrases and acronyms bounced around during conversations. To help you navigate through them I've compiled a short list of common terminology that you can expect to encounter when dealing in paranormal matters and in general conversation.

Abominable Snowman: The Abominable Snowman is reputed to be an ape-like cryptid which is taller than an average human being. They are believed to inhabit the Himalayan region of Nepal and Tibet. In addition to being called the Abominable Snowman, they are sometimes called the Yeti and Meh-Teh by the people indigenous to the region. It is also believed they are in some way connected to the Big Foot phenomenon, either directly or indirectly.

Akashic Records: The Akashic Records are thought to be a compendium of all human events, all thoughts, all words were ever spoken, all emotions expressed and felt, and all intent ever to have occurred in the past, present, or future. They are believed to be encoded in a non-physical plane of existence known as the etheric plane. An excellent metaphor for this would be the world-wide-web or internet which contains the total sum of all human knowledge, even all future knowledge. It is believed that since time isn't linear, the past, present and future have already happened, and are still happening. Therefore, the Akashic Records are a way of accessing data about things in our plane of existence no matter where or when they will happen, are happening, or have happened. There is a good deal of anecdotal evidence their existence, and a great many people believe in the Akashic Records. However, no scientific evidence is so far available to categorically support their actual existence.

Alien: The word “alien” commonly refers to an extra-terrestrial being or intelligent life that does not originate from planet Earth. So far, they are still only hypothetical life forms because no indisputable public proof has been made available about their existence. However, their existence is highly likely, even if only statistically.

Angels: An angel is a supernatural being common in various religions and mythologies. In Christianity, angels are typically depicted as being benevolent celestial beings who act as intermediaries between God and/or Heaven and Humanity. It is believed by some that angels often undertake the role of protectors, guiding human beings and carrying out God's tasks. In Christian-based religions, angels are often organized through the taxonomy of a certain hierarchy. They are frequently given specific names and/or certain titles. For example, Angel Gabriel is sometimes called the "Destroying Angel".

The concept of angels in religion and folklore dates back thousands of years, and even today we don’t really know much about them. Many people today believe in their existence and that they can receive help and protection by making requests directly to certain angels. Some people claim to have seen angels, and that they walk amongst us. However, theologians say they are typically invisible to us because they are spiritual beings, and therefore rarely take on a solid physical appearance.

Other people are more sceptical. They believe that if angels existed, they were probably extraterrestrial beings that were badly observed and documented by the primitive people at the time they were recorded. As such, they would only be able to write about them and record them according to whatever common frames of reference they had to work within. Hence the representations of angels and "fiery" flying chariots might be a common frame of reference for benevolent extraterrestrial beings using flying machines, personal propulsion systems, and/or spacecraft.

Anomaly: An anomaly is a deviation from the normal, the common order, or the rule. Something that deviates from what is standard, normal, or expected.

Apparition: An apparition is technically a form of supernatural appearance of a person, or entity. The term is typically associated with the appearance of a ghost or wraith which seems to possess some form of physical substance so that it is either seen, heard, detected by smell/scent/odour, or even by touch.

Ball Lightning: Ball lightning remains an unexplained atmospheric electrical phenomenon which refers to luminous spherical objects. These can vary greatly in size from the size of a small berry to many feet in width. Ball lightning is especially associated with thunderstorms and lasts much longer than a lightning bolt. This suggests they may be composed of a form of plasma. It has been reported on several occasions that ball lightning eventually explodes, and it can even have fatal consequences to those who are near it when it does. There are reports of ball lighting leaving behind the scent of sulphur and/or ionised air after it has disappeared.

Banshee: A banshee is said to be a female spirit in Irish folklore/mythology whose wailing or shrieking sound heralds the death of a family member. The name "Banshee" is connected to the reputed importance of tumuli, or mounds, which are common in the geographical topography of the Irish countryside.

Baseline Readings: Establishing a set of primary baseline readings is basic to all kinds of experimentation and investigations. In paranormal investigation, these involve the measurements of the location, the electromagnetic energy, the time, general temperature, specific temperatures at certain spots, humidity, geomagnetic activity, barometric pressure, compass function/anomalies, gasses such as carbon dioxide, and carbon monoxide, etc.

Big Foot: The Bigfoot or Sasquatch in North American folklore is a hairy, ape-like being which walks upright. It is reputed to live in the wilderness of North America and often leaves behind large footprints from which it derives its common name. It's most commonly associated with the Pacific Northwest, but they have been reported in many other areas of thick forest and wilderness. The Big Foot is the North-American equivalent of the Yeti.

Chupacabra: The Chupacabra is a mythical creature in the folklore of parts of Northern and Southern America. It was first reported as being sighted in Puerto Rico, and the creature derives its name from the apparent habit of attacking and drinking the blood of livestock, especially goats and sheep.

Clearing and Smudging: Clearing, or smudging as it is also known, is the action of clearing a location or person of lingering energy. The energy that is cleared is typically said to be negative, evil, or generally bad. In its place, positive energy is then invited to fill the void. The process and action of clearing/smudging usually involve the burning of sage together with prayers, incantations and injunctions. The action is said to be made effective due to the 100% belief and intent of those performing the process. The process is also associated with exorcism.

Cold Spots: A cold spot in paranormal investigation is a supposed area of abnormal localized coldness. It can also be a sudden area-specific decrease in ambient temperature. It is believed that when this happens it is directly connected with paranormal activity.

Cryptozoology: Cryptozoology aims to prove the existence of mythical entities such as Bigfoot, and also animals which are thought to be extinct. These entities are commonly referred to as cryptids. Cryptozoology is still considered to be a pseudoscience.

Demons: A demon is a supernatural malevolent energy entity in religious and occult texts, as well as in the mythology and folklore of many parts of the world. A demon is thought to be a harmful spiritual entity which exists outside "heaven" and both in and out of "hell". It is believed that it is possible to summon a demon through certain incantations and rituals and that once conjured it can to a certain degree be controlled.

Devil, Satan and Beelzebub: The Devil is the personification of pure evil in many cultures throughout the world. In the Christian religion, the Devil is the Hebrew Satan or the primary opponent of God. In Christianity, the Devil was created by God, and therefore is essentially the counterbalancing dualist opposite of God. The equivalent balance of negative energy to counterbalance the good energy.

Satan is an entity of the Abrahamic religion, and in Christianity, it is depicted as being a "fallen angel". Satan is reputed to offer temptations to humans to stray them away from good. In Christianity, Beelzebub is another name for the Devil or Satan. In demonology, Beelzebub is one of the seven princes of Hell and is capable of flying. Therefore, Beelzebub is also known as the "Lord of the Flies".

Doppelganger: A doppelgänger is the "look-alike" or double of a living person, and in some traditions as a harbinger of bad luck. In other folklore, a doppelganger or "double-goer" is believed to be someone's evil twin. Interestingly, American President Abraham Lincoln is believed to have encountered his doppelganger which is seen by many to have foretold his assassination.

Dowsing: Dowsing is a form of divination typically used in attempts to locate underground, buried gems, objects, metals or graves, etc. The only equipment a person would use to dowse would be either rods or sticks. Dowsing is still considered to be pseudoscience because there is no current scientific evidence/data to support that it is any more effective than pure random chance.

Ectoplasm: Ectoplasm is associated with the manifestation and apparition of spirits. It is also a substance thought to be emitted by mediums who communicate with the spirit world. The term “ectoplasm” was originally used to describe a substance "exteriorized", or physically manifested/produced by mediums.

Elementals: An elemental is a type of mythical magical entity which personifies a force of nature. It is said to be able to control the natural powers derived from their associated element. The concept of elemental entities is associated with ancient mythology, folklore and religion.

EMF: EMF, is an abbreviation for either an Electromagnetic Field or an Electromagnetic Frequency. Almost every natural thing either living, animate, and even inanimate, will emit some sort of electromagnetic field. It is theorised that certain paranormal entities, and especially ghosts and spirits, emit, react and respond to electromagnetic energy. Therefore, it is believed that these entities can be detected by using Electro Magnetic Field (EMF) meters.

Entity: Technically, an entity is something that exists as itself, as a subject or as an object. This might be either physical or not, which covers the abstract variety of entities. Since an entity describes something with its own form of existence, if it exists, then it’s an entity. In paranormal terms, the word “entity” is used to describe things that exist, but which we know little or nothing about.

Epicentre: An epicentre is a focal point, confluence, convergence, or central location. In paranormal terms, an epicentre is the point at a location, or the person, or the specific object which is central to the phenomena.

EVP: An EVP, or Electronic Voice Phenomena, is the capturing and recording of voices and sounds that are not generated by humans, other known living beings, or from natural sources. It is believed that some paranormal entities communicate at a level/frequency/pitch which is inaudible to the naked human ear. However, this can be recorded via a microphone and heard when played back.

Exorcism: An exorcism is the religious and/or spiritual practice of clearing/driving out/evicting paranormal entities which possess a living person, object, building, or location. The entities which are most commonly exorcised are believed to be demons, and/or various forms of negative energy. An exorcism may be performed by causing the entity to commit to swearing an oath to leave, often through an elaborate religious ritual. Alternatively, it may be performed by simply commanding it to leave, usually in the name of a deity or higher power, dependent upon the belief of the exorcist. The process is only made possible by 100% committed belief and intent on the part of the exorcist. Exorcism is connected to smudging.

Fairies: A fairy is a type of paranormal/mythical entity associated with European folklore. They are usually classed as being forms of "elementals".

Foo Fighters: The term "Foo Fighter" describes a type of UFO which was frequently seen by many Allied aircraft pilots during World War 2 in the skies over both the European and Pacific theatres of operations. They usually appeared as luminous glowing objects which could travel at incredible speeds. They seemed to defy laws of aviation and mass/inertia by almost instantly performing abrupt stops, turns and manoeuvres.

Today, it is believed by many that they were a form of alien drone which was used to observe and communicate data about the war to extraterrestrials.

Genii: Genii is the plural of genie. Genie is the English translation of jinn from the original Arabic. A genie is a supernatural entity in Arabian/Islamic mythology. In French, "genie" refers to any kind if spirit.

Geobox: A "geobox" is a proprietary type of ghost box/spirit box used to communicate with paranormal entities. Basically, it is a type of modified portable AM/FM radio that continuously scans many different bands in the hope of directly communicating with a ghost as it does so.

Ghost Box: A ghost box is a radio receiver device that rapidly scans multiple radio frequencies to attempt to communicate with spirits/ghosts. They are also known under proprietary names as either a Frank's box, or a Geobox. During operation, they typically generate a great deal of "white noise" and audio remnants from local broadcast stations. It is believed that paranormal entities can manipulate the frequencies to create words and entire sentences to communicate with investigators. It is recommended that audio recorders should be attached to and used in conjunction with these devices to record any evidence which might be obtained during an investigation.

Ghost: It is believed that a ghost is the soul/spirit of a dead person or animal, that can appear to the living, and sometimes interact with them. Ghost descriptions vary from being a simple invisible presence, translucent/barely visible shapes, vaporous forms, to realistic life-like apparitions. Some are even said to have been able to manifest in almost solid form.

Ghost Lights: Ghost lights, earth lights, spook lights, and will-o'-the-wisps, are luminous balls/spheres of light, often seen to be moving and/or blink. They are primarily seen outdoors and have been reported from all parts of the world. Scientists believe that they are most likely caused by some sort of natural occurrences, such as marsh gas. However, it remains unknown as to how it forms and behaves in the apparently intelligent ways that it has been witnessed and recorded by many people over the years.

God: God is believed to be the supreme being and the principal object of faith. God is described as omniscience, omnipotence, omnipresence, and as having an eternal existence. God is believed to be the benevolent creator of all things and is the direct opposite/opposing force to the Devil and everything evil.

Haunting/Haunted: A haunting or a haunted place is a location where there is apparent paranormal activity, and as such is frequented by a ghost/s and other entities.

Incubus: An incubus is a "Lilin-demon" which is in male form. In myths, legends and folklore an Incubus will lie on top of a sleeping woman to engage in sexual activity. Some societies believe that repeated sexual activity with an incubus result in the general overall debilitation of the victim, and even death.

Leprechaun: In Irish folklore, a Leprechaun is a small, mischievous sprite which is a specific type of fairy of the "Aos Sí" in Irish folklore. Like other Irish fairies, Leprechauns are possibly from the Tuatha Dé Danann. Curiously, Leprechauns rarely appear in older Irish mythology, only in the more recent. They're typically depicted as being small bearded men, wearing a coat and hat. It is believed that if captured by a human, they often grant three wishes in exchange for their freedom. It is also believed that they have a hidden pot of gold at the end of rainbows. There are believed to be links between fairies, aka "the little people", and leprechauns.

Loch Ness Monster: The Loch Ness Monster, or "Nessie" as it is frequently affectionately known, is an aquatic being which reputedly inhabits Loch Ness in the Scottish Highlands. It is often described as being very large, with a long neck and one or more humps protruding from the water. If it exists, it is possibly some sort of dinosaur that didn't become extinct such as a plesiosaurus or similar.

Manifestation: A manifestation is a clear appearance of a ghost, spirit or other paranormal entity in bodily form. It is very similar to an apparition in that a manifestation can typically be seen, touched, heard, and/or detected through smell.

Medium: A medium is a person who can communicate with and/or channel spirits and/or ghosts. Someone who communicates with ghosts and "the other side" as it's commonly called. A medium is thought to be able to communicate with discarnate entities, which are intelligent entities with no physical body.

Mel Meter: A Mel Meter is a multi-purpose combination unit that measures EMF, temperature and other data simultaneously. It was designed by Gary Galka of DAS Distribution Inc. after the sad loss of his daughter Melissa, to which she lends the device part of her name. I write more about this interesting story in a later chapter.

Since it is commonly believed that ghosts/spirits can manipulate EMF energy, and since heat is also a form of energy, then when it's transferred from one location to another it leaves behind a cold spot and EMF energy traces. The Mel Meter is designed to register both AC/DC EMF fluctuations together with recording variation/fluctuations in temperature on a single display in one unit. They are highly recommended as being both useful, well made, and very reliable by many professional paranormal experts.

Mothman: The Mothman is a mythical cryptid native to West Virginia in the United States. It is said to be half-human and half-bird/moth with enormous wings, grey-brown in colour, and over 7-feet tall. The Mothman was reportedly seen in the Point Pleasant area of West Virginia between November 12, 1966, to December 15, 1967. After the Silver Bridge collapsed on December 15, 1967, killing 46 people, it gave rise to the legend which directly connected the Mothman sightings to the bridge collapse, and as being general harbingers of disaster. Many UFO experts, paranormal investigators, and cryptozoologists believe that the Mothman which was witnesses at that time was, in fact, an alien. Other believe that it was a supernatural manifestation or an unknown species of cryptid.

Ouija Board: A Ouija board is also known as a "spirit board" or a "talking board". Typically, it is a flat board with the letters of the alphabet marked on the surface together with numbers 0–9, and the words "yes", "no", and occasionally they will have both "hello", and "goodbye". There are often several additional symbols and graphics marked on the board as well. The board is used through the people using it holding a small heart-shaped piece of wood or plastic called a planchette. All those participating in the Ouija board session will place their fingers lightly on the planchette and it is moved about the board to spell out words. This is supposed to be without those touching the planchette consciously pushing it to influence its movement and deliberately create words.

Spiritualists and some paranormal investigators believe that the dead can contact the living via the Ouija board. Many Christian denominations have warned against using Ouija boards because they can lead to demonic possession. However, some occultists are divided on the issue. Most occultists reiterate the warnings of the many Christian religions and caution against Ouija board use. From the evidence we've seen directly, and from several other sources we trust, we'd strongly caution against Ouija board use by anyone except the most experienced paranormal professionals and mediums.

Operation of the Ouija board is broadly similar to the glass-and-table divination technique. The glass-and-table divination technique involves each member of the group surrounding the table and placing one finger very lightly on the rim of a down-turned glass that positioned in the middle of the table. Questions are then asked, and any responses are made by requested specifically directed movement of the glass around the table.

Orbs: Orbs are spheres of translucent light that seem to occur in areas with reported paranormal activity.

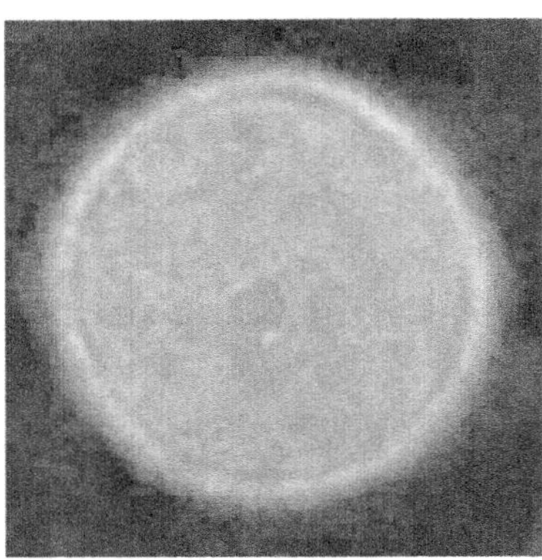

It's now known that almost all commonly videoed or photographed orbs are a most likely a phenomenon of dust or insects captured due to a quirk-combination of wide aperture lenses, focusing systems, and certain digital imaging sensors.

However, as always seems to be the case when it comes to paranormal investigation, there is the annoying 5% (ish) of orbs that cannot be rationally explained-away and seem to be intelligent entities.

Orbs in the annoying 5% (ish) that cannot be rationally explained, and which appear to have intelligent control to move, stop, and change speed/trajectory while others around them float freely, are believed by many to be a spirit or ghost. These are frequently be captured in photographs taken in alleged paranormally active locations.

A huge well-defined orb I captured during an investigation on the banks of the Mississippi River near St. Anthony Main, Minneapolis, Minnesota, USA.

My co-investigator next to the orb is Curt Hansen who is about 6 feet tall and weighs about 200lbs.

Ovilus: The Ovilus, or Puck as it is also known, is a device with electronic speech-synthesis capability. The original device was created by a retired electronics engineer called Bill Chappell. They work by harnessing electromagnetic activity in combination with a computer dictionary and a voice synthesis mechanism. The Ovilus is well thought of and seen as a valuable and reliable tool by paranormal professionals.

Paranormal: "Paranormal" is generally accepted as being anything which is outside the realm and experiences which are deemed to be "normal". The term is often used to describe a wide variety of things such as ghosts, UFO's, cryptids, aliens, fairies and many other phenomena that alleged exist and yet defy traditional scientific explanations.

Physical Manipulation: Physical manipulation is when an object is allegedly moved or physically altered by a ghost, spirit or another paranormal entity. Physical manipulation would include lights switching on and off, and objects moving without any human action. When a torch is used in paranormal investigation and a ghost or spirit apparently communicates via the medium of turning it on and off, then this would be classed as a form of physical manipulation.

Psychokinesis: Psychokinesis, also known simply as PK, is apparently a technique of mind over matter through invisible means. It is also known as Telekinesis, and examples of PK/Telekinesis would be the movement of objects, bending metal, and determining the outcome of events. Psychokinesis is a term for any ability involving the manipulation of matter and/or events with the mind alone.

Poltergeist: A Poltergeist in both folklore and in parapsychology is a type of ghost or spirit that is responsible for physical disturbances, such as loud noises and objects being moved or destroyed. The name, "poltergeist" is from the German for "noisy ghost" or "noisy spirit", and they frequently knock on walls and doors.

Poltergeists are apparently able to physically attack humans through pinching the skin, biting, leaving bite marks, punching, striking, hitting, pushing and/or tripping. Poltergeist activity generally also includes the movement and/or levitation of objects such as furniture and cutlery.

It has been observed that poltergeist activity often centres on and around certain individuals such as teenagers, and especially teenage girls. Scientists who have investigated poltergeist activity believe that it may be caused in part or whole by hormonal changes linked to triggering a form of latent uncontrolled telekinetic ability. It is believed that this telekinetic ability is within all humans, but it is typically latent. However, some people have been reported to be able to use their telekinetic ability at will

Portal: Portals and paranormal doorways are believed to be ways in which paranormal entities can enter our reality/dimension. They are allegedly a form of invisible gateway between our earth and other realms/worlds/dimensions. They are theoretically linked to wormholes and the wormhole theory in astrophysics.

Possession: Possession is when a person, animal or object is allegedly taken control of by another energy being/spirit/entity/demon/the Devil etc. it is most commonly believed that possession is usually by a demon. Most of the world's religions accept possession as being real and have specific processes to deal with it should it occur.

If the malevolent entity has taken control of a person, then typically they will act completely out of character. Often, they will speak in languages which they have no previous knowledge, appear to physically change in various ways, or speak in voices which are apparently not their own. There now seems to be some scientific basis to support how the mechanism of possession can take place. I write more about this in a later section in this book about the dangers involved in paranormal investigation.

PSI: PSI is about parapsychology which is the investigation and study of paranormal and psychic phenomena. This would include telepathy, precognition, clairvoyance, psychokinesis, near-death experiences, reincarnation, apparitional experiences, and other paranormal abilities and conditions.

Psychic: A psychic is someone with the apparent ability to use extrasensory perception to identify information which is hidden from the normal accepted physical senses we possess. A person with psychic ability will typically use a combination of telepathy and clairvoyance. Such a person can perform acts of revealing hidden information that is inexplicable to the currently accepted laws of physics. The term/word "psychic" would also cover parapsychic ability and metaphysics. A psychic is believed to be able (in part) to access the cosmic consciousness and Akashic records. As you'll have already read in chapter 1, there is now some scientific evidence that people can actually read the mind of other people and be connected to the greater mass of human consciousness.

My wife Helen has a degree of psychic ability in that she can "see" things in advance during our everyday life which then come true. One example of this was when we were driving towards Big Lake, just North of Minneapolis, MN in the United States. As we passed the house of one of her friends, Helen suddenly exclaimed that she had a vivid image of police cars outside the house and also in the driveway. However, at the time we drove by there were none. Later that evening Helen received a phone call from another friend who had just driven by the same house where Helen had "seen" the vision 30 minutes earlier. Her friend then asked if she knew why there would be several police cars with flashing lights outside their mutual friend's house. It seems that as we passed by Helen had been able to "see" 30 minutes into the future when the event would eventually take place.

On another occasion, Helen told me details of a vision she had in advance of a paranormal investigation we were going on later that day. We were to investigate The Terrace Mill in Glenwood, Minnesota, USA in September 2017. While meditating, Helen had envisioned that during our investigation we would encounter the spirit of a man who had his arm severely injured through accidentally being caught in machinery in the building. Later, when the investigation was eventually concluding, the curator of the mill read our group selected sections from an old journal which had been displayed in one of the glass showcases in the building. She told of how a man who was buying the business was being trained in its operation by the old owner. That was when the new owner had a terrible accident causing his arm to be badly injured, and it was the only accident that had ever occurred at this Mill. This was exactly as Helen had envisioned 9-hours earlier that day.

Residual Energy or Haunting: Residual energy and a residual haunting are explained by two possible events taking place. One is a "playback" of a past event that has somehow been recorded in the fabric or structure of the location. This would connect the phenomena in some way to the "Stone Tape Theory". It is also theorised that a residual haunting might involve the warping of space-time and be an audio-visual porthole to observe events which occurred at a different time. A portal in time somehow opens to allow past events to be re-witnessed in some sort of time-loop under the right conditions.

When encountering residual energy and a residual haunting, typically there is no current connection or communication with a paranormal entity/spirit. It is theorised that emotionally-charged events leave a sort of residue or imprint of their energy behind. This can then be somehow “played back” when circumstances are conducive.

With a residual haunting, the event being witnessed will repeat itself almost exactly every time, with no changes and no interaction possible with whoever or what is involved in it. A residual haunting could be both visible and/or audible. For example, noises such as footsteps or knockings may be heard with no visual apparition.

Revenant: A revenant ghost is believed to be a deceased person returning from the dead to haunt the living. They appear as either a full-body apparition able to interact with the living, or only audibly or visually. This phenomenon is related to the concept of a spirit called a “fetch”, which in Irish folklore is the spirit of a person who is still alive, and therefore the double of a living person.

Séance: The word "séance" is French in origin, and it is an attempt to communicate with spirits that are either deceased or that only exist as energy-form entities. Today, it commonly refers to people who are gathered together to receive messages from ghosts, or to listen to a clairvoyant/spirit medium converse with and/or relay messages from paranormal entities and/or spirits.

Shadow People: Very little is known about shadow people. They're typically witnessed as dark figures, often as fleeting glimpses through the corner of the eye. It is unknown if they are malevolent, benevolent, or impartial.

Smudging: Smudging is a ceremony that involves the burning of herbs such as sage, together with the spoken words of blessing and cleansing. Smudging is like an exorcism in that in paranormal terms it means to rid a place of negative or evil energy/entities. However, on most occasions, smudging or cleansing will be performed for no other purpose than to clear out the nominal negative energy, and it isn't because a place is haunted by a malevolent entity or demon. As with exorcism and prayers of protection, the power of smudging doesn't come from the herbs that are used, rather from the absolute intent of the person performing the smudging and the person who owns the property who also believes in that power. Therefore, many different herbs and things can be used to smudge, or cleanse/clear a place, because they are simply the focus for the intent to be transmitted through.

Spirit: The word "spirit" is from the Latin meaning "breath" or "to breathe" and is the non-physical part of a person which is the seat of emotions and character, as well as the soul. In paranormal terms, typically a spirit is a supernatural being such as a ghost, fairy, or other entity. The concept of a spirit is directly connected to the concept of spiritualism.

Spiritualism: Spiritualism is the belief that the soul/spirits of the dead exist and can communicate with the living. Spiritualists believe that the afterlife, or "spirit world", is a place where spirits continue to evolve in some way. It is also believed that spirits are somehow more advanced than humans, and through the surmised ability to more easily connect to the "cosmic consciousness", they can see into the future. There are some basic scientific arguments which could support the possibility of this. This is because we now know that time isn't a linear process of cause to effect, and instead, it is jumbled with numerous interconnections. Some spiritualists believe in the concept of "spirit guides" which are specific spirits that are relied upon for spiritual guidance and well-being of a person.

Stone Tape Theory: The Stone Tape theory was first proposed by British archaeologist turned parapsychologist Thomas Charles Lethbridge in 1961. The official label of "Stone Tape" derived from the title of a 1972 BBC drama by Nigel Kneale (18 April 1922 – 29 October 2006) who was a British screenwriter. He famously created the character "Professor Bernard Quatermass" of the BBC and Hammer Film Productions between 1953 and 1996. In doing so, he typically brought science together with the paranormal to create some landmark movies which at least in part, had some validity in science.

It is theorised that ghosts and hauntings can be recorded in the physical structure/matter of a building or location. This is in the same way that we can make video and audio recordings on tape which is designed for the purpose. The theory supports the electrical mental impressions released through deeply emotional and/or traumatic events can somehow be "stored" in the surrounding physical matter. Once the information is stored/recorded, then under the right circumstances it can be “replayed” and witnessed by people in future times. It is believed that certain physical materials such as wet rock, limestone, and metals are better at “recording” than other material. This is in the same way that certain material is better when used as the fabric of audio and videotape.

Both limestone and granite are thought to have paranormal qualities and be capable of absorbing and recording energies, events, sounds, and images according to Stone Tape Theory. This is because the most likely proposed mechanisms for the recording and playback of the immediate surroundings primarily involve quartz, calcite and aragonite (which are different crystal forms of calcium carbonate), and iron oxide. These materials are also believed to be involved in the quantum entanglement of particles and recorded electromagnetism. Granite is an igneous rock composed of between 20% and 60% quartz by volume, and at least 35% of feldspar, with minor amounts of mica, amphiboles, and other minerals. The word "granite" comes from the Latin “granum”, meaning a grain, and refers to the grained structure of the rock.

A classic example of what is either a stored recording, a glimpse back into time, or a combination of both, was first reported by a man called Harry Martindale. Harry was a young heating engineer’s apprentice in 1953 when he saw about 20 Roman soldiers march through the cellar wall past him while he was working in the old

Treasurer's House in York, England. The Roman soldiers were only visible from the knees up, and this would suggest a time-loop or "stone tape recording" of some sort. This is because the old Roman road they appeared to be walking on is actually a few feet below current ground level. The soldiers he witnessed didn't interact with him in any way and didn't even appear to see him.

It was as if he was either looking at a vision of some kind of "recording" being replayed, or he was looking through a wormhole in time, or a one-way viewing portal. Interestingly, the apparition was seen after Harry Martindale had been working away vigorously hammering and drilling through the stone wall. Perhaps this was the trigger needed to activate whatever it was that was necessary for him be able to either look back in time or to play back the recording in the fabric of our reality.

Succubus: A succubus is a Lilin-demon in female form and the counterpart of the male Incubus. In folklore, the paranormal/supernatural entity appears in dreams when it takes the form of a woman to seduce men into sexual activity. It is commonly believed that repeated sexual activity with a succubus results in severe debilitation of the victim and affect the health and/or mental state of the person, possibly even leading to death.

Tarot Cards: The tarot is a pack of cards, similar to playing cards. They have been used since the mid-15th century in various parts of Europe, and from the late 18th century onwards they began to be used for divination and fortune-telling.

The tarot has four suits which vary by geographic region. The regions are the French suits used in Northern Europe, Latin suits in Southern Europe, and German suits in Central Europe. Each suit has 14 cards. They have 10 pip cards numbering from one (Ace) to ten, and four face cards being the King, Queen, Knight, and Jack/Knave. They have a separate 21-card trump suit and a single card known as the "Fool". The Fool may act as the top trump or may be played to avoid following suit.

Divination using playing cards is recorded as far back as 1540, with the earliest evidence of a tarot deck being used for this purpose from a manuscript dated from around 1750. This documented the rudimentary divinatory meanings for each of the cards.

There are specifically occult tarot card decks dating from around 1789. These contained themes related to ancient Egypt due to the mistaken belief that such cards were derived from the Book of Thoth.

The 78-card tarot deck has two distinct parts with the first 22 cards being the Major Arcana (greater secrets), the second being the Minor Arcana (lesser secrets) consisting of 56 cards.

Experienced diviners who use and interpret tarot cards believe that the future is fluid which makes absolute predictions impossible. Therefore, they only focus on possible outcomes and influences related to the issues at hand. Therefore, Tarot readings should not be seen as being a guarantee of any ultimate predicted outcome/s.

This "fluidic" interpretation of the future is in line with the scientific concept of Schrödinger's cat theory. The theory devised by Austrian physicist Erwin Schrödinger in 1935 is a paradox and basically states that every possible outcome of an experiment exists. Schrödinger's cat theory is related to the many-worlds interpretation of quantum mechanics that implies that all possible alternate histories and futures are real, each representing an actual world or universe.

Telepathy: Telepathy is the supposed transmission of information from one person to another without using any of our known physical sensory channels, or through any form of physical interaction. There is new scientific evidence to support the possibility of telepathy since it has now been discovered that all human brains are connected and interconnected by a low-level energy field.

Temporal Distortion: A temporal distortion is a fictional form of a quantum singularity. This is used by writers to refer to a range of phenomena which resemble a gravitational singularity in that they are a massive, localized distortion of space and time. Since the term was first written in science fiction, it has since become synonymous with general anomalies in time and space. As such, when people have allegedly witnessed events which appear to be back in time, they are termed as being either temporal distortions or temporal anomalies.

As I mentioned under the section about Stone Tape theory, an example of this phenomena could be when Harry Martindale witnessed the Roman soldiers marching through the cellar of the Treasurer's House in York.

Technically, the term "temporal distortion" represents a fundamental problem in physics, namely the difficulty of making Einstein's theory of relativity merge with quantum mechanics. This is because according to the theory of relativity, a singularity is very small, and quantum mechanical in nature. So far there is no theory of quantum gravity that has been conceived.

UFO's: An Unidentified Flying Object or UFO is a flying object that is not readily identified. The majority of UFO's are eventually rationally identified as being either conventional objects or known phenomena. However, there are many which have been reported by members of the military, police, and civil aviation authorities that defy rational explanation. The term "UFO" is widely used for alleged observations of extraterrestrial craft.

USO's: USO's or Unidentified Submerged Objects are simply any objects that are of unknown origin which are observed underwater, and which remain unexplained even after a thorough investigation. These are the marine equivalent of a UFO, and they are much more common than it was first believed. This shouldn't be too surprising due to the enormity of liquid volume on our planet. The oceans are so vast that even today they can't be effectively monitored.

Voodoo: Voodoo has many different names and spellings. These include

- Vooodooo
- Vodou
- Voudou

- Vudu
- Vodun
- Vodoun
- Vundun
- Vowdown

Voodoo is the name of a West African spiritual folkway, and many believe it to be a religion. The essence of Voodoo is always a spiritual folkway passed from generation to generation via oral tradition, the practice of rituals, and routine spiritual practices. It travelled to the American continent from Africa and found homes in the Caribbean and the deep south of the United States.

Voodoo is often used to frighten, and its practices are frequently portrayed as being evil. This perception has been enhanced and perpetuated through the media and movies for many years. A Voodoo doll is an effigy into which pins are inserted. It isn't only related to Voodoo, because such practices are also found in the magical traditions of many other cultures around the world.

Vortex: A vortex is allegedly the centre of focused or concentrated paranormal energy. A vortex therefore typically refers to a type of mysterious disturbance in the fabric of space and/or time. It is believed that they are an opening/portal/wormhole to another realm or dimension.

Wand. A wand sometimes referred to as a magic wand, is typically a thin hand-held stick made of either wood, stone, bone or metal. In witchcraft, Wicca, Shamanism and other types of ceremonial magic the practitioners use wands to focus and channel their energy.

Wicca wands are most often made from wood such as Hazel or Oak, and usually, represent the elements of fire or air.

Wiccan: A Wiccan, or Wicca (Pagan Witchcraft), is pertaining to a Pagan religious movement, and developed in England during the early 20th century. Wicca draws upon ancient pagan theological structure and ritual practices.

Witch: A witch is a woman who is thought to have magic powers. They are usually depicted as being evil powers, although not always. A witch is popularly depicted as wearing a black cloak, a pointed hat, and with the ability to fly on a broomstick. The word "witch" is possibly related to the English words wit, wise, and wisdom to mean that it would be the "craft of the wise".

It is believed that witches differ from sorcerers in that they don't use physical tools or actions to curse. Instead, their maleficium is perceived as extending from some intangible inner quality. Maleficium is a Latin term which means "wrongdoing" or "mischief", and it typically describes the malevolent, harmful magic, and "evildoing" of witchcraft or sorcery.

Witchcraft: Witchery or wizardry is the practice of and belief in magical skills and abilities. Witchcraft is a religious divinatory and/or medicinal art which is often present within societies and groups whose cultural framework includes a magical worldview.

The concept of witchcraft and the belief in its existence have been recorded throughout history. Scientifically, the existence of witchcraft and magical powers are believed to lack evidence because they aren't supported through experimental laboratory testing.

However, individual witchcraft practices and their effects on others might be open to scientific explanation or be explained via psychology and the subsequent power of belief. This is a little like the placebo effect in medicine where the placebo is equally efficacious as the drug simply because the recipient believed it to be so.

Witchcraft is often believed to influence the mind, body, or property of others against their will, although this is not always the case. Some people believe that the malefic nature of witchcraft is a Christian projection designed to scare people away from it so that they only follow Christianity.

Warlock: A Warlock is a man who practises witchcraft, and who is a sorcerer. The male equivalent of a witch.

Wormhole: A "wormhole" is a common term for what is technically an Einstein–Rosen bridge. An Einstein–Rosen bridge is a hypothetical topological feature that would be a shortcut connecting two separate points in spacetime.

Therefore, at least in theory, a wormhole could connect to extremely far distances of billions of light years or more, or it could connect extremely short distances of just a few feet. An Einstein–Rosen bridge could also theoretically connect different universes together as well as different points in time.

Chapter 4: Basic Equipment for Paranormal Investigations

In the world of paranormal investigation, there are many phrases, terms and acronyms for equipment that may initially sound a little confusing. Even experienced professionals can get confused because items are being developed and launched with increasing frequency to capitalise on this fast-growing market sector. In paranormal investigation, and especially when it comes to ghost hunting, investigators typically use a wide variety of devices. To help you navigate through the maze of what's available to buy, I've prepared a list of the most popular, and what we believe are the most effective pieces of equipment. The fact is that you don't need a lot of equipment to ghost hunt, and you certainly don't need to break the bank either. In addition, you may even already own some useful items which you can use.

EMF AKA Electromagnetic Field Meters. EMF meters are "standard equipment" for all paranormal investigators. They detect and measure the intensity of electromagnetic fields. It's believed that the presence of anomalous electromagnetic fields is an excellent indicator of paranormal activity, and particularly the presence of ghosts. K-2 meters are just one type of such device.

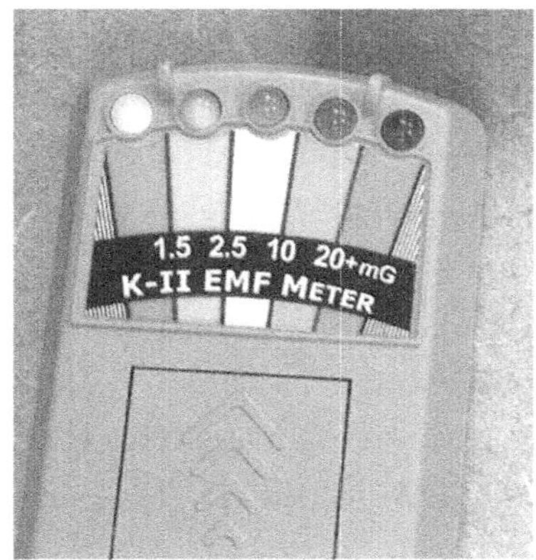

These devices also help to eliminate the contamination of evidence through inefficient electronic equipment and hidden power cables. There are several different styles of EMF meters on the market and they basically all do the same thing, so the choice is yours.

Some types of EMF meters require calibration, and if you have one of these then make sure that you deal with this matter before beginning an investigation. Since these devices are generally inexpensive and effective, then professional investigators usually have several of these devices in their equipment bag.

There are some EMF meters which have a digital display. However, most have some form of spring-loaded needle and dial, or an LED light array (from left to right) of green, yellow, orange, and red. Green would indicate the lowest level of intensity and red the highest. These devices can be easily deployed and often left alone during an investigation. Since they have a highly visual light display, if they detect the presence of any abnormal activity they can be easily spotted. Some devices also have an audio tone to accompany the increasing level of EMF intensity.

If you're holding an EMF device during an investigation then I'd suggest holding it at about waist height, slightly in front of you. Also, to avoid making any rapid movements, especially waving your arms around. A rapid movement will produce inaccurate readings, so beware of this in advance, and don't make this mistake.

Before you start investigating, always take and note baseline readings from all the places you plan to investigate. Then, when you next take readings in those places if you notice a sudden spike in EMF levels, then you have a baseline comparison to check it against.

If you detect EMF activity, then in a similar way to using a metal detector, I'd always suggest that you follow the spikes and high-level readings. It's worth always remembering that if you suddenly register an EMF spike, then it is more likely to be a man-made anomaly rather than paranormal activity. Try not to jump to conclusions, and always investigate scientifically and thoroughly. For example, if you're experiencing an EMF spike near the floor, then double check for hidden and recessed electrical cables connecting light fittings and junction boxes in the room on the next level below, and also within walls and the cladding of supporting beams and pillars.

This very thing happened to a team I was part of when we were investigating The Terrace Mill in Glenwood, Minnesota, USA in September 2017. Fortunately, they were a very well-trained and experienced team, so they didn't jump to any conclusions despite the sudden dramatic EMF spike the team registered. After registering the first of several anomalous EMF spikes, together with some other highly unusual EMF activity, they began a rigorous process attempting to logically eliminate potential sources of infrastructure contamination. Eventually, they found that in the room below there were hidden electrical cables and junction boxes recessed in the cladding that was not obvious to a superficial visual inspection of the structure. The process of elimination required them to study the detailed plans of the building and to speak with the owners about structural work that had been done to ensure the structure met local council building codes, etc. Finally, don't forget to record all the EMF data you get for a thorough comparative analysis later.

Digital Stills Camera. A good digital stills camera is another basic staple needed for all types of paranormal investigations. Make sure that you have a big enough memory card and take a spare along with you just in case. Before the investigation, make sure that you clear off any old data stored on the memory card so that you don't run out of space for image files at a critical moment.

Batteries and battery life are always a limiting factor on long investigations, especially since you'll be frequently using battery-draining flash photography. If your camera only has an internal rechargeable battery, then once the initial battery charge has expired your camera becomes nothing more than an ornament. Once this stage is reached, even if you take the precious time-out of investigating to return to base camp and plug the camera into the mains to recharge it, you're still without a camera until it has been fully recharged, which will normally be several hours.

If your camera uses a special battery that is specifically designed to only fit your camera, then since you'll almost certainly need spares, they must be ordered in advance. More importantly, special batteries are usually very expensive when compared to ordinary batteries.

The best kind of digital camera to choose is one which uses readily available batteries. They'll probably be a little more expensive to buy initially, but you'll save much more than the initial expense factor in the long run, and you'll be a better prepared paranormal investigator. With a camera that uses readily available batteries, then when you run out of power during an investigation you're only going to be out of operation for as long as it takes you to swap out the old batteries for fresh ones.

You never know precisely when you'll have the opportunity to capture the definitive evidence needed which will be the pinnacle of your career. The evidence that will rocket you into the media limelight as being "the person who proved the existence of ghosts". The greatest shame would be to have such a moment spoiled because your camera had run out of batteries and you couldn't recharge it or replace them in time!

Technically, the more pixels the camera has, the higher the resolution the pictures will be. Also, the greater the dynamic range of the camera, then the better and more detailed the images that you'll capture. Dynamic range or the DR/DNR of a camera is the ratio between the largest and smallest values that a certain quantity can assume. Or in slightly less technical jargon, the ratio of maximum measurable light intensity to the minimum measurable light intensity. Why is it important to have a camera with the best dynamic range possible when performing paranormal investigations? The answer is simple. Paranormal investigations are almost always performed in no/low light scenarios and environments which generally challenge most cameras. The more challenges which your camera faces, then the images you capture as evidence will be less detailed and of lower quality. The better cameras with the widest dynamic range possible will yield images which show little or no digital noise or pixelation. The important details you need will be amazing, which are usually hidden within the blurry shadows of pictures taken on lesser cameras.

Camera Modifications. Some video and stills cameras can be retrofitted to capture images in a much wider electromagnetic spectrum than just regular visible light. However, if you can find somewhere to modify the camera, it is usually a costly procedure. Therefore, it's recommended to simply buy a camera that has been specifically designed for this purpose. Today, full spectrum video or stills cameras aren't prohibitively expensive.

These cameras enable images to be captured which would normally not be visible to the naked eye. This is important since we don't really know which part of the bandwidth of electromagnetic radiation a ghost or paranormal entity will register in. We shouldn't simply assume that everything will be visible within the comparatively small spectrum of visible light that we see with the naked eye. Furthermore, we still can't even be certain if we know all there is to know about the wider EM spectrum in general. Who knows what science will discover tomorrow which will suddenly change all the "hard" rules of today which we once thought to be the pinnacle of human knowledge.

There are currently 9 known types of electromagnetic radiation which fall into the following categories:

1. Gamma radiation
2. X-ray radiation
3. Ultraviolet radiation
4. Visible radiation
5. Infrared radiation
6. Terahertz radiation
7. Microwave radiation
8. Radio waves

At one end of the electromagnetic spectrum there is ultraviolet (UV) and infrared (IR) in each of their respective bandwidth clusters. Around the section where the near ultraviolet light meets the near infrared light, we get the comparatively small bandwidth of visible light. Beyond that, you get the mid and far infrared light extending into the microwave and then radio wave bandwidths onwards.

We all know that light travels in straight lines. Therefore, when the light hits an object it is reflected/bounces off the object at the same angle that it hits. This process of light being reflected off objects is how light enters our eyes, and this is how we "see" the object.

Visible light is made up of different wavelengths, with each wavelength being one colour. Therefore, the colour we "see" with our eyes is a result of certain specific wavelengths of light that are reflected back to us. Objects appear to be different colours simply because they absorb some colours or wavelengths of light and reflect or transmit other colours. The colours that we see are simply the specific wavelengths of light that are being reflected/transmitted back to our naked eyes.

For example, a red ball looks red to us because the molecules of dye pigment in the material fabric have absorbed the wavelengths of light from the other parts of the spectrum. Therefore, red light is the only colour of light that is reflected from the ball. If only a violet light is shone onto a red ball, then it would appear to be black. This is because the violet light would be absorbed by the ball, and there would be no red light to be reflected.

This simple process could explain how certain paranormal entities, UFO's, and even cryptozoological creatures are able to hide from detection with the naked eye. They may be there right in front of us, but if the type of light that our eyes can detect isn't reflected off it, then we won't be able to see it. Therefore, paranormal professionals use a wide range of detection equipment including cameras that can "see" and record images across the entire electromagnetic spectrum.

Video Cameras. Most of the same rules and wish-lists of capabilities and qualities that apply to digital stills cameras also apply to video cameras. However, it's almost certain that a video camera will only use its own proprietary type of battery system, so it simply won't be possible to use regular batteries as an option. Whatever type of batteries your camera uses, always be sure to buy the ones which have the largest capacity, and to have plenty of spares.

It's a good idea to buy a system which you can get battery charging systems that allow more than one battery to be charged at the same time. These options are typically only available for the more professional cameras, but as with all things in life, you generally get what you pay for. I once worked for a considerable time with BBC TV, so despite being sorely tempted at this point to begin writing lots of technical stuff about TV and video resolution, I'm going to keep it all nice and simple.

You should always get the camera with the highest resolution and the best dynamic range in the class you can afford. Today there are many 2K and 4K camera options to choose from. 2K video gives you 1920 X 1080 lines of resolution and 4K gives you between 3840 X 1600 and 4096 X 2160 lines of resolution. The latter figures being those of the Digital Cinema Initiative. Some professional camera models now offer 6K and even 8K resolution, but these still aren't commercially common or practical for most people.

When selecting a camera for paranormal investigation, as well as considering factors such as resolution and dynamic range, there is also the signal to noise ratio (SNR) which should be considered. The signal-to-noise ratio is a physical measure of the sensitivity of a cameras imaging system. The visible "noise" in a video or stills picture is the digital equivalent of the graininess of film. Digital images display noise as random specks on a picture that would otherwise be smooth with cleanly defined images. The more noise in a picture, the more the quality of that picture is degraded. The amount of noise in a picture will increase as you electronically increase the sensitivity setting of the camera. The better the chipset and imaging sensors/processors that a camera has, the better the camera will naturally be able to handle the darker and more challenging lighting situations without adding undue noise into the picture.

Some cameras have built-in infrared light (IR), and can easily switch between operating in the visible light spectrum into IR operation at the flick of a switch. However, most wide/full spectrum cameras on sale today require an additional camera-top IR or UV light. These additional lights in those spectrums may be worth considering even if your camera has a built-in IR or UV light. The more powerful light will enhance the effectiveness of a built-in camera light that comes as standard. The bigger the light on the camera then the greater the distance it will be able to see objects and record them clearly on video.

Make sure that the lenses of all stills and video cameras are checked for dust contamination before an investigation. If they require cleaning, then ONLY use a microfibre lens cloth to clean them with. NEVER use anything else unless you want to ruin the lens of your camera by adding micro-fine scratches to the lens that tissue or ordinary cloth material will cause. If you don't always use a microfibre lens cloth to clean your lenses, then you'll be creating your own contamination to any visual images you capture. Naturally, this isn't a very professional thing to be doing if you want to be taken seriously as a paranormal investigator.

When you first deploy a video camera, I always prefer to set it recording and then stand in front of it to "mark" the recording. Marking the recording is when you say on camera where you are, what you're doing, the day/date, where the cameras are, what camera number it is and any other data that might be applicable. You can always support this "marking" onscreen by holding a written sheet of paper stating the same details. This is in a similar way to how professional TV and film crews use the marker, or "clapper" board to mark a shot.

Don't forget that the addition of a high-quality microphone can greatly enhance the evidence you capture with a video camera. The better video cameras allow a professional audio connector to be connected. These are known as XLR cables and the most common type have three pins and a circular connector. They deliver balanced microphone and line-level signals over long distances. If your camera doesn't have the ability to directly connect an XLR cable, or if you're using a digital stills camera in video mode, then you'll need to buy a 3rd party adaptor to allow their connection. These are easy to get from professional video dealers, and the best types have the option to supply phantom power to certain professional microphones that might need it. Never skimp on audio equipment, it is often the opinion of many TV professionals that the most important part of a good video is good quality audio.

When it comes to analysing video footage after the investigation, you'll need to invest in some good video editing software. This will allow you to see the video and audio tracks on a timeline so that you can zoom right into the track at a single frame level. This will also allow you to review, edit and enhance any EVP's that have been captured during the video recording. I'll cover more about recommendations for both audio and video editing software in a later section.

If you want to capture the best evidence possible during your investigations, then you cannot compromise on the quality and capability of your stills and video cameras, and any audio equipment that attaches to them.

A video timeline together with the audio waveform in Adobe Premiere video editing software

Thermal Imaging Cameras. Since objects and people emit different temperatures, these cameras will allow you to see these displayed onscreen in different colours. The hotter colours will be displayed as yellow, orange and reds, the cooler colours as blues into blacks, and the neutral temperature is generally green. You can now get some excellent dedicated thermal imaging stills cameras and/or thermal imaging video cameras.

Since it is believed that paranormal entities, and especially ghosts, can draw energy from around them these devices will theoretically be able to help you detect that process taking place. Therefore, a cold spot would develop in a place where the heat was being drawn from, and a hot spot would form where energy is being concentrated. These cameras may need time to calibrate before operating them, so take this into account before using one.

Digital Audio Recorder. A digital video recorder should be part of your standard equipment list for any paranormal investigation. These excellent devices allow you to effectively capture EVP's, or Electronic Voice Phenomenon. When selecting a model, it's a good idea to buy one with the greatest storage capacity you can afford. It's basically the same rule as for when you buy memory cards for your video and stills cameras, bigger is always generally better. In addition to noting the amount of data storage the device will allow, also check the projected battery life of the device. Again, the greater the battery life, the better the device will serve you when deployed. The best devices allow for the connection of additional external microphones if needed, and they'll also have some form of a USB connector to link into your computer.

You'll also need software on your computer which allows you to visually see and playback the audio waveform, so remember to take this into account when you buy a device. Again, I'll cover more about recommendations for both audio and video editing software in a later section.

Ovilus. The Ovilus is an excellent device to have with you on any investigation. Depending upon which model/type you're using, theoretically, it uses a wide range of different sources to communicate in "real-time" with paranormal entities, and particularly ghosts. An Ovilus might draw information from sources that include, electromagnetic fields, scanning multiple radio frequencies, and microwaves.

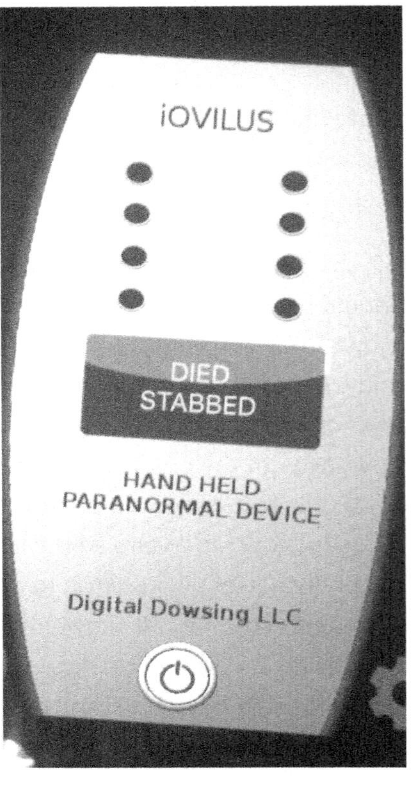

The Ovilus works through what is technically known as "Instrumental Trans-Communication" which is the name given to this technique by the German physicist, Professor Ernst Senkowski. He also named the technique of contacting with paranormal entities/ghosts using any electronic method to capture and record the voices and the images of ghosts. This is what is more commonly known as an EVP, or Electronic Voice Phenomenon.

In theory, ghosts may contact you of their own volition if an Ovilus is left running, or they can directly respond to your questions that are asked. An Ovilus will always be limited to the dictionary that is built into the software to display the text. In respect of playing back or relaying voices, then the device may have words pre-recorded into a database, or it will work independently of a dictionary by relaying them as an assembly of letters phonetically. Again, this all depends upon the type of device you choose.

Different devices offer a range of different settings, so it's a good idea to note precisely which settings you use if you make significant contact with something. It's still unclear if and/or how these devices are affected by other elements such as barometric pressure, radiation of various kinds, and temperature etc.

There is Ovilus and Ovilus-type software that is available for mobile phones, tablets, and computers. If you use these on any of those devices, or anything else which can transmit or receive electronic signals, then this leaves them open to contaminations. If you use this type of software on these devices then always turn off all modes of transmission, wi-fi, and cellular operation. Flight mode is a good way to turn off your mobile phone easily. However, even with these devices all turned off in respect of transmission and reception, there is still no guarantee of eliminating cross-contamination of whatever you pick up or connect with on them.

It should be noted that since there is no hard science in how the Ovilus communicates with paranormal entities, then accordingly whatever they capture cannot technically constitute "proof" of anything. Whatever you capture might be real, or it might be complete nonsense, the fact is that no one really knows. Even the original creators of the early devices once labelled them "entertainment purposes only", so draw your own conclusions from there. I see them as being a useful tool in a wider arsenal of devices that are better used in coordination together rather than as stand-alone devices.

Motion Detectors. These are useful and inexpensive devices to have with you during any paranormal investigation. Naturally, they work in all lighting conditions, which is a huge benefit when exploring at night. I always feel that it's better to use them in conjunction with a video camera which can hopefully record the visual images of whatever it is that causes the motion detector to activate. Some of the better devices have a choice of different types of alarm noise they emit when activated. By choosing a specific alarm noise for each location that you deploy one, it will make it much easier to identify where you should direct your attention if one is triggered. Otherwise, if they all emit the same sound, then you and your team will initially be confused about where to look. Running around in the dark to check different locations could contaminate other evidence being gathered.

Hanging Bells and Wind Chimes. These are another simple and inexpensive device that can be deployed during your investigation. Naturally, they'll be useless in places where there is a strong draft or in the open air, but they are OK when used inside a reasonably well-sealed building. Basically, they make a crude, yet highly effective motion detector.

The Electrostatic Meter. Naturally, this device will detect static electricity from several sources including clothes, shoes and electronic devices.

It is theorised by many paranormal investigators that ghosts emit an electrostatic charge and can affect these devices which detect it. These devices fall very much into the category alongside motion detectors. They're very useful, and even though any detections they might make on their own aren't indisputable evidence, it might be when it is viewed as part of a much wider range of evidence that has been collected.

Since many types of fabric in all types of common clothing generates some degree of static, they're very susceptible to outside contamination. Therefore, if electrostatic meters are used during an investigation, then make every attempt to discover all possible logical causes if any are activated.

The Mel Meter. This is an excellent device which is reliable and will accurately monitor a wide range of sources

on a single display screen. They are professionally built, well-constructed, and accurately calibrated, which is why many professionals use them during their investigations.

As I mentioned earlier, the Mel Meter was developed by a gentleman called Gary Galka after the sad loss of his oldest of three daughters, Melissa. Soon afterwards, the family noticed that some highly unusual things began happening in their home. This was when Melissa began to let the family know that she was still there and that she was reaching out to them in these unusual/unconventional ways.

Gary Galka owned a company called DAS Distribution Inc. which was a well-established supplier of precision industrial non-contact and contact measurement devices and data gathering systems. This is how he was able to design and develop such a high quality, accurate monitoring device.

He designed the first Mel Meter to communicate with his daughter Melissa, and the rest is history. Melissa gave her name to the device, the model number was the year of her birth which was 1987 (87), and the year of her passing being 2004 (04), to give the Mel-8704. She was just a youthful 17 years old when she passed.

Gary Galka has developed over 30 other devices that can be used for paranormal investigations. Using his Spirit Box he recorded his daughter saying, "Hi Daddy, I love You." He voluntarily kindly donates a substantial portion of his company profits from the sale of paranormal detection equipment to various bereavement support groups.

Compass. The simple magnetic compass is an inexpensive addition to your growing paranormal toolbox of equipment. Since a compass is obviously affected by magnetic fields, and since some believe that ghosts and other paranormal entities either emit or can affect magnetic fields, then their presence could alter the direction of a compass needle. When you use a compass always take note of which direction the needle is pointing if you suddenly pick up any deviation or if it begins to spin. During your initial walkthrough of the location that you're about to investigate, make sure that you pinpoint any location or devices that are there which can cause a compass to malfunction. This will be important during the evidence processing phase when you try to find all possible logical benign reasons for the device to malfunction instead of immediately jumping to a "paranormal conclusion".

Fishing Bobbers. Again, these simple devices are a useful add-on to your equipment bag. Since the best devices have a small flat base area, they are very sensitive to movement and vibration. Therefore, in theory so long as there is no outside contamination to affect them, then if one is caused to fall from the position it was placed in, this could be an indication of paranormal activity.

Laser Grid Torch. A laser torch which emits an interlocking grid-type of a beam is a very useful and inexpensive tool. As you probably already know, the word "laser" is an acronym for Light Amplification by the Stimulated Emission of Radiation.

When either a single beam or an interlocking grid-type of a beam is projected into an area you're investigating, if anything breaks that beam by crossing it, even if it cannot be seen with the naked eye, you will see that the beam is broken when it does so.

If you're using an interlocking grid-type of a beam, then the size of whatever breaks the beam could theoretically be estimated by the amount of disruption to the gird. You can also use a single beam laser pointer to "spot check" an area if needed.

The devices can be clamped to a camera tripod or attached with gaffer tape if you don't have a clamp. This way the camera can record anything that disrupts the laser grid it emits. However, for best results, if you position the laser grid pen behind the camera, you'll widen the effective range of whatever the camera captures.

The laser grid works best in darkness while indoors. For safety reasons, they're always best used at a low level, across a corridor or entranceway rather than directly through it. These laser devices are safe when in contact with bare skin, but they are extremely dangerous to the naked eye. NEVER point any type of laser or any other type of strong light source directly into the eyes. Also, never use them directed through additional lenses such as spectacles, telescopes, or binoculars. Any contact with the naked eye can cause irreparable damage and even complete blindness.

Torch/Flashlight. Aside from their obvious function of making it possible to see in areas of total darkness, torches (AKA flashlights in the United States) are widely used by many paranormal investigators.

They typically use the small Maglite type of torch which works by twisting the head where the bulb is housed to turn it on. When they have twisted it just enough to light it up, they will then very slightly twist it in reverse to just turn it off. They do this because it is believed by many investigators that ghosts can manipulate energy. Therefore, they can make a connection between the two electronic contact points inside the torch head to make it either light up or turn off according to their will.

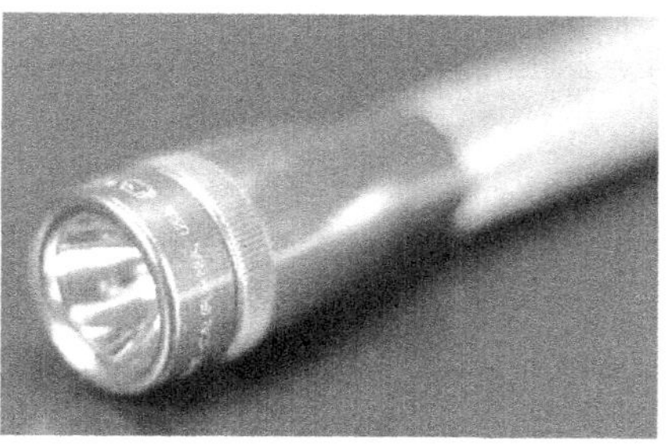

I've been on many paranormal investigations where an apparently coherent conversation has taken place between an unseen entity and the people asking questions. A question has been asked, and if not immediately, then within a reasonable period of time the torchlight has either turned on or turned off to answer the question. It really has been as if there were a direct question and answer session taking place between the investigators and whatever it was they had apparently made contact with.

However, I have serious doubts about the overall reliability of using a torch in this way. I often feel that any evidence obtained through these sessions should be treated with more scepticism than evidence gathered through more reliable methods.

I'm not saying that every session that has taken place using a torch has been a waste of time. Far from it. I'm sure that many sessions have contacted an entity that has been able to use the torch as a means of communication. However, I'm equally certain that on many occasions there have been sessions where the supposed "contact" was nothing more than the torch lighting up and turning off due to simple material science issues.

Most of the older types of Maglite use a traditional incandescent bulb in the torch. When the bulb is lit, it naturally emits heat inside the case of the torch. The heating will cause expansion, and this could turn the torch on or off depending upon its switch design. Similarly, even when the torch is unlit it is still susceptible to temperature changes in the room you're using it in. There is also the question of atmospheric moisture and the electrical conductivity of the air within the casing of the torch which must also be considered.

If you're going to use a torch as a means of attempted communication, then always use one with an LED bulb which will generate less heat than an incandescent one. Personally, I'd be much more impressed if a ghost was able to operate a regular model torch with a switch that you had to depress to turn it on or off. To many, I may sound more like a sceptic after that last sentence. However, I'm not, I'm simply being objective.

I suppose that you either like using a torch to gather evidence, or you don't, the choice is yours. Either way, having a few good torches together with plenty of batteries available during any paranormal investigation will always be useful. At least they'll help you to avoid getting bruised shins, banged knees and even broken noses from walking into objects in the dark.

Used Batteries. Whilst on the subject of torches (flashlights) and batteries, I thought I'd mention how even "used" batteries can still be useful. Even though a used battery may not be powerful enough to power a torch, they still have some power left within them. You can always save your old batteries and bundle them together.

When the batteries are clustered into a bundle, a ghost might be able to use some of the collective residual energy to make contact in some way. Using the collective residual energy, they might be able to communicate via EVP, knocking noises or perhaps even by an apparition. It may be a long shot, but I believe that it's well worth trying. Besides, you can feel happier about doing your "bit" in the worldwide campaign to recycle everything possible!

Night Vision. Night vision glasses/goggles can be extremely useful because unlike a torch (flashlight) they don't cause potentially damaging light pollution. Night vision equipment will allow you to see in almost total darkness by amplifying whatever light is available. However, the less light, the greater the screen image "noise" and graininess will be.

The better night vision equipment will have an infrared option will allow you to see in total darkness. Since the equipment will project infrared light, even though this is invisible to the naked eye, it will be visible to full spectrum video and stills cameras. So, beware of contaminating them by using night vision equipment in areas where these cameras are deployed.

Many seasoned paranormal investigators especially like using night vision glasses because a great deal of activity seems to take place within that part of the electromagnetic spectrum.

Tri-Field Meter. These devices are very much like the Mel Meter in that one device can detect multiple types of emissions from various sources without any physical contact taking place with the device. Typically, tri-field meters have a squelch mechanism built in, and only measures natural energy, meaning that it blocks out electrical wires, and pipes etc.

Laser Digital Thermometer. These are excellent tools which are very useful during any paranormal investigation. Since you're able to point a laser beam with great accuracy over long distances to take a temperature reading, this device will always be a winner! When using one, be sure to first set the device to register either in Celsius or Fahrenheit, whichever is your preferred choice of measuring temperature.

Since it's theorised that ghosts and other paranormal entities can cause the temperature to either rise or fall, then these wonderful devices take accurate multiple readings from a variety of different spots within seconds of each other.

Walkie Talkies. These are extremely useful when investigating almost any location. They allow you to keep in touch and communicate information etc. without physically traipsing around to pass messages which will always cause some degree of noise and other contamination. They also avoid the need to use cellular devices to send texts or make calls which might affect other equipment. You get what you pay for, so don't buy cheap ones. The better units operate over greater distances, they don't easily break up speech due to cheap electronics, and their batteries will last longer.

Barometer. Since it's now possible to buy small, inexpensive, and reliable barometers with a digital display, then I believe they're worth deploying on a paranormal investigation. If, as it is sometimes theorised, ghosts can affect barometric pressure by either raising or lowering it, then this is another excellent tool you can easily carry with you. It could register some interesting supporting evidence.

It's important to note that if there is a thunderstorm developing in the area where you're investigating, then both a barometer and an ion detector will be affected by this. Thunderstorms ionise the air, and the barometric pressure will drop significantly, so please take these factors into consideration when noting down any readings you gather.

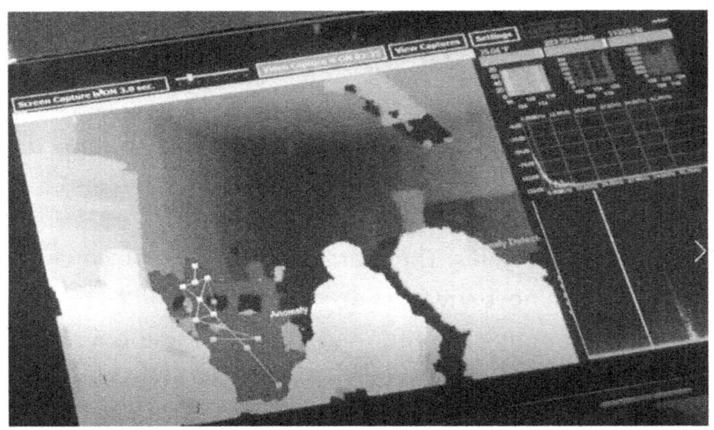

A typical SLS Kinect screen. Note the anomaly slightly centre-left between the two people seated.

The SLS Kinect Camera System. The system is commonly known simply as "SLS", and the portable version which is typically used in most paranormal investigations was originally developed by techno-genius, Bill Chappell.

The SLS system harnesses an RGB (Red, Blue, Green primary colours) camera and an infrared light projector which projects thousands of tiny dots which allows the computer to "see" everything in 3D-depth sort of like radar/sonar, even in the dark.

The SLS Kinect system can analyse and detect the distance between the camera and object, together with a thermal image. The screen also displays certain data-metrics such as distance and temperature etc. This system makes it very easy to record video and audio of whatever it captures. This Includes the onscreen data-metrics which are encoded right onto the hard drive as a video file on the tablet or computer the system operates on.

An SLS system can be used either hand-held on a gun-like mount, or on a fixed tripod, and it can be used with either battery or mains power.

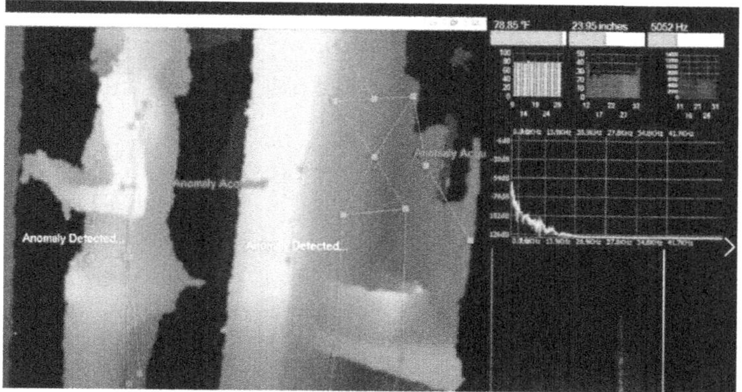

On this SLS Kinect screen note the anomaly slightly centre-right, and the person slightly centre left.

Wax Paper. Regular kitchen wax paper is a very inexpensive method of detecting footsteps from unseen feet. Simply deploy it in certain areas where there will be no foot-fall from the team during the investigation and leave it there. Any footprints that are placed on it are easily visible, and if it's unused then it can be rolled up and reused at another time.

First Aid Kit. A good first aid kit should be standard equipment on any investigations, and it should expand to adapt to any special requirements as needed. Expansion and adaptation over and above the standard kit should come when investigating in outdoor and remote locations, and if any scuba diving might be involved. In scuba operations always bow to the knowledge and requests of the divemaster and dive team leader. Always keep your first aid kit locked and in a cool, dry environment, out of the reach of children. Items to include in your kit are as follows:

- Sticking plasters (band-aid type) in a variety of different sizes and shapes.
- Sterile gauze dressings in small, medium and large sizes.
- A minimum of 2 sterile eye dressings.
- Triangular-shaped bandages.
- Crêpe-style rolled bandages.
- Safety pins and clips.
- Disposable sterile gloves of the non-allergenic type.
- Tweezers.
- Scissors.
- Alcohol-free cleansing wipes.
- Sticky tape.
- Gaffer tape.
- A thermometer, preferably digital.
- Skin rash cream, such as hydrocortisone or calendula.
- Cream or spray to relieve insect bites and stings.
- Antiseptic creams.
- Painkillers such as paracetamol, aspirin (which is not to be given to children under 16), and ibuprofen.
- Superglue.
- Cough medicine.
- Cold medicine.
- Antihistamine tablets.
- Distilled water for cleaning wounds.
- Eyewash and an eye bath.

A basic first aid manual and instruction booklet should be kept with the first aid kit. All medicines should be regularly checked to make sure they are within their use-by dates. Ideally, everyone on the team should be first aid and CPR certified. However, if this isn't possible, then at the very least, one person in each team should be qualified in first aid and CPR.

Conclusion. The list of possible equipment you can use in a paranormal investigation is always going to be as long as you want it to be. Many seasoned investigators will have their own add-ons and special devices which they like to use. Remember, to begin with, you don't have to spend a fortune to get started, but you will need some basic equipment. I'd suggest that you simply buy more equipment as you find the need for it arises, and to always stick to the basic staple devices first.

The plain truth is that no one can say with any degree of certainty that ghosts will emit "X" or respond to "Y". Even today, everything is still nothing more than an educated guess in this respect. You will also find that certain equipment works better on one investigation in certain conditions, whereas other equipment will produce better results at other times on other investigations.

Finally, it should always be remembered that there's a big difference between an educated guess and a gamble. A gamble is always down to pure chance where you cannot influence the outcome in any way. Whereas an educated guess is an informed guess which is based upon your knowledge, experience, and previous experimentation.

Chapter 5: Where to Find Ghosts and Potentially Paranormal Active Locations

When people first become interested in the ghost hunting aspect of paranormal investigation, one of the first things they think about is what are most likely locations that might be haunted.

One of the first locations that usually comes to mind is a cemetery. Oddly enough these places tend to be the least haunted places. Cemeteries may look spooky, but typically they aren't high on the list of places that are frequented by the spirits of the deceased. When you think about why this is, it makes complete sense. If, as is theorised, we continue in spirit form after our physical death, then if we're able to return to the world we left, why would we return to a gloomy cemetery? That would certainly be the last place I'd choose when I could theoretically go anywhere I desired. Wouldn't it make more sense to return to somewhere we once loved in life, or to revisit our loved ones again? This doesn't mean that there are no paranormal entities frequenting cemeteries because there is evidence of this. It seems there are a variety of entities who are well aware of where they frequent.

The reality is that "ghosts" can probably be found anywhere. This is because there are no hard rules that we know of about where they can go or can't go. Therefore, in theory, the choice of where a ghost frequents is entirely the choice of the ghost in question.

Since paranormal activity can occur almost anywhere, start somewhere convenient. For example, you may pass by a piece of open land and/or a new building every day in a city such as Manchester, England as you travel to work. On the face of it, there is nothing there in the open space except grass, and the new building is bright, clean, shiny, and not in the least bit "spooky".

I know of just such a place on Wilmslow Road, just as you pass the Platt Lane junction as you head into the city in Manchester, England. However, I also know that many years ago at the same location there was a very old theatre, which was demolished back in the early 1980s. In addition, there were several shops and other old buildings including a funeral parlour located there.

I also know from my grandmother that on the same site prior to the theatre there was a much older music hall and bar in the mid-19th century, which had been demolished to make way for the early 20th-century theatre. I clearly remember my grandmother telling me that her mother and even her grandmother had once told her that on the same site they knew of a famous murder which had taken place, and also about people being killed in a fire in one of the buildings which were once there. Therefore, even though today there is nothing there except a seemingly innocuous and innocent small section of grass, a flowerbed, an advertising hoarding, and a shiny new car dealership next to it, a lot once happened there. That small patch of grass and flowers and the shiny new building are set in a place that has an extremely interesting history, and one which might cause paranormal activity to take place there.

The point I'm making is that just because there might be nothing there now that would suggest it was a classically paranormal active location, don't automatically dismiss it because you have no idea what happened on that same location over the years, and in the air above ground where the old buildings once stood. In a country as old as Britain, and other countries of similar age or older, there are numerous potentially paranormally active locations.

In newer countries such as the United States, the same rules apply, although you'd never get to see something like a "stone tape theory" recording of Roman Legions walking past you like those that have been reported in England. I'll try to give you a better perspective of just how old some of the buildings are in Britain. To do this, I'll briefly describe what happened when my wife Helen, who is from the United States, took a tour of York Minster with me. When we were in the lower basement of the building looking at the foundations, the tour guide told us that even though the large parts of today's structure date back about 2,000 years, York Minster was built over the top of a much older temple dating back about 2,500 years. Also, there were buildings there before that. My wife was literally speechless.

When we go on paranormal investigations in her native Minnesota, I always smile to myself silently when the apparent "great age" of a building is mentioned. During countless pre-investigation briefings we've been told that "This building is very old, it dates to 1880!" Old? A place built in 1880 isn't really that old. The house I lived in as a child dated back to 1850, and there are lots of those all over Britain still today. When people perceive a building from about 1880 as being old, they're only comparing it to everything else around them in a country which habitually demolishes and rebuilds every few decades. They've simply either lost or never really had a balanced global perspective on what constitutes old or not.

In the United States, it is often forgotten that even a 400-year history since the British first settled Plymouth Colony is actually not really a long time in world terms. The native American people have an illustrious heritage on the continent for much longer than that. We also know that the Viking explorers penetrated deep into the continent from the time the "Viking Age" began around 800AD to 1066AD. It's also highly likely that the Knights Templar also made trips deep into the heartland of North America from around 1119 onwards. In addition, DNA testing of Native Americans indicates a large percentage of them have Western Eurasian and Western European ancestry. This was probably made possible because of the early land-link attachment across the now Bering Sea which we call Beringia and the land-link which was formed by ice sheets between Europe and North America.

The point I'm making here is that no matter what country you live in, no matter how "young" or "old" it's considered to be, people have been living, loving, giving birth, fighting, murdering, waging war, and dying there for many thousands of years. So just because a place you know well during your lifetime has been nothing more than grassland, or something equally benign, it doesn't mean that nothing ever happened on that site. Far from it, most likely things have happened there that would make your mind "boggle" and surprise you. So, keep an open mind about all places and buildings in respect of the potential paranormal activity. You simply never know what you might find if you dare to look!

Potentially Paranormally Active Locations

To help fire-up your creative thought "juices" about where to search out places which harbour potential paranormal activity, I've listed a few of them down. I've also described why they might be paranormally active.

Mental Health Hospitals. These places always seem to be highly active, especially the older hospitals. I remember filming on several occasions at the Kirkbride State Hospital which is a mental asylum near Fergus Falls in Northern Minnesota, in the United States. This is a huge old abandoned building that sprawls out above and below ground for several acres. It even had its own mortuary, crematorium and cemetery on the same site. From the moment you enter the building, you can sense a strange energy and activity taking place there, and this was

The Kirkbride State Hospital, Fergus Falls, MN.

almost always verified by the equipment we were using. After interviewing former medical staff and other people who had worked on the site for many years, it seems that some hideous events took place there. These include someone who was mistakenly boiled alive in a warm water therapy pool. The result of the mistake was terrible for the poor victim because they were boiled to the point where their skin had come away from their body and was floating in the water around a completely cooked human being. Other atrocities included barbaric lobotomies and electric shock treatment that would have driven even the sanest of people completely crazy.

Another excellent location to investigate is the Waverly Hills Sanatorium of Duluth, Minnesota which is more commonly known as the Nopeming Asylum. Like the asylum in Fergus Falls, the Nopeming Asylum is highly paranormally active and well worth a serious investigation. Since I hardly think that both the Kirkbride and Nopeming Asylums are unique in these respects, I'd highly recommend that mental health hospitals are either high on, or right at the top of any list. If imprints of extreme emotion and the recordings of hideous deaths can be somehow recorded into the fabric of the structure, then these places must surely be crammed with data galore. In addition, who knows how many lost and tormented souls have never found their way out of such places?

Prisons. Abandoned prisons must also rate very high on the list of potentially paranormally active locations for similar reasons to mental asylums. Prisons aren't places where the cream of humanity is sent for the good of their health. Instead, they've typically housed the lowest of human scum imaginable. Murders, rapists, paedophiles, and possibly even worse, have all been incarcerated in these buildings. Inmates have been frequently beaten, regularly raped by each other, and experienced unimaginable tortures over the centuries.

There have also been many completely innocent people who have been wrongly incarcerated, and either left to die a lingering death, or agonised while waiting to be executed for a crime they did not commit. Therefore, prisons in general, have been filled to the brim for centuries with the most extreme emotional energy.

The main entrance to Bodmin Jail in Cornwall, England.

Bodmin Jail. Bodmin Jail, which is also referred to as Bodmin Gaol, is an imposing former prison situated in the sleepy town of Bodmin, Cornwall, England, right on the edge of the mysterious and sometimes sinister Bodmin Moor. It was built with an estimated 20,000 tons of Cornish granite, quarried on Bodmin Moor and completed in 1779 by Napoleonic prisoners of war.

It should be noted that both limestone and granite are believed to be a key component of the phenomenon known as Stone Tape Theory. This is when the fabric, or material structure of a place or building, somehow "records" and/or absorbs emotional and other energies, events, sounds, and images present in the immediate environment. Therefore, Bodmin Jail is an estimated 20,000 tons of potential Stone Tape Theory recording material that has housed some of the most extreme emotional energy imaginable for centuries.

Bodmin Jail remained a working prison until it eventually closed in 1927. In recent times, Bodmin Jail was heavily featured in the hit BBC television series Poldark from 2015 onwards as one of the important filming locations. Between 1785 and 1909, fifty-five people were executed at Bodmin Jail, and except for four, all hangings were performed as grisly public executions. In those days, the public perception of capital punishment was very different from how we typically perceive it today in modern western countries. Back then, it was very much a spectator event, with hundreds, if not thousands of people gathering together to watch someone being executed.

Of the four hangings that were not public executions, two took place on a side-balcony scaffold within the jail, and two in the purpose-built execution pit. This is still there today, and it forms part of the tour when visiting the jail. Interestingly, the last man to be hanged in the jail's execution pit was William Hampton in 1902, who was also the last man to be executed in the county of Cornwall.

To get a more complete overview of the history of Bodmin Jail and the paranormal activity that takes place there, we were very fortunate to connect with the resident paranormal expert, Kirsten Honey. Kirsten is not just a historian and expert in the paranormal, she is also someone who is psychically gifted. This meant that we were able to get a detailed overview of what had taken place there, the recorded paranormal activity, and the suspected psychic energies present in the jail.

Kirsten Honey kindly consented to an interview and told us about some remarkable occurrences and apparitions that have been recorded in the jail and surrounding grounds. We now know that several tourists who were simply visiting the jail for no other reason than because it's a great thing to do, have captured some unexpected, mysterious, and completely baffling faces and figures in their photographs and selfies. There have been so many reports of people being grabbed or pushed while climbing or descending the narrow winding stairways that it is strongly impressed on all visitors to never use the stairs unless they always use the handrail, just in case...

There are frequent sightings of a man and a woman, but not usually together, in the same area of the jail. This is just inside the main gate on the right-hand side, not far from where the execution pit is. There are also many reports from visitors of the sounds of children playing, and occasionally of apparitions of children. This isn't surprising, because many children were once jailed for what we would now not even consider being a crime. Also, a man could be jailed for debt and his entire family would be incarcerated along with him.

During paranormal investigations, and after-hours ghost walks at night, the sound of the execution pit lever being operated has frequently been reported and recorded. Also, the sounds of footsteps on the gravel, and even occasional voices. Interestingly, there have been many reports of what appears to be an "intelligent" haunting. This is because stones seem to have been specifically thrown at certain places such as the waste bins and specific signs, probably to attract the attention of who was there at the time.

Since I was a guest speaker at the official 2018 Paranormal conference held at Bodmin Jail, along with the extraordinarily knowledgeable and entertaining speaker and author, Jason Semmens, we were fortunate to be allowed a VIP behind the scenes tour. This allowed us to perform a full preliminary investigation during the daytime, which is something we consider to be essential before undertaking any overnight investigation. A couple of days later, after the conference had been concluded, we performed a comprehensive overnight investigation. We were joined by Bodmin Jail's resident paranormal expert, Kirsten Honey, fellow guest speaker Jason Semmens who is one of the leading authorities on witchcraft, and a few other people who had been specially selected to participate in forming the two teams that we needed.

As well as using various electronic testing and measuring devices, we used the Ouija board and the glass-and-table divination technique as our primary methods of attempting to contact whatever entities might be present. We were not disappointed. Our first experiment involved a selected group of people and the Ouija board in a 1st level basement room which was once an old prison cell. The rest of us positioned ourselves just outside the small circle of people who had volunteered to place a finger lightly on the planchette. They also kept their eyes closed to avoid any subconscious movement of the device in any specific direction. The people surrounding them operated an Ovilus, an EMF detector, a video camera and a DVR.

Sam Barkham, who is a paranormal expert and guide at the jail, began asking the initial questions as we attempted to open-up communications. It wasn't very long before the planchette began to move around the board quite freely. However, for this group, when a question was asked and the planchette responded by moving to hover over certain letters of the alphabet, the combination of letters didn't make any sense. It was not even close to communicating with an entity that might have once been an illiterate human being who had little-to-no education during their lifetime. In fact, I even commented aloud that it was more akin to a game of anagrams, and perhaps we should call in the team from the TV show 'Countdown' to help decipher the message, if there was one.

Therefore, we ended that session and each team then swapped positions so that new people could operate the planchette. It wasn't long before the new people were getting intelligent responses from the planchette. However, after a comprehensive question and answer session, Sam Barkham and I both independently reached the same conclusion. This was that we seemed to be dealing with some sort of non-human, yet non-the-less highly "intelligent", entity that was possibly malevolent.

At this point, I took over the questioning and politely but firmly directed whatever it was we had connected with, to answer my new questions. I demanded to know what kind of entity it was, what was its point of geographic, dimensional, or time-space origin, if it had a name, and what its intent was. I also demanded to know if it was under the command of another entity, or not. This was when it became increasingly agitated, almost angry and aggressive in its apparent frustration in either being repeatedly asked these questions, or in being either unable or unwilling to answer them. There were several occasions when the planchette was being almost flung around the board in extreme agitation. It eventually became clear that whatever it was we were dealing with wasn't going to reveal itself. So, we concluded the session and our entire team relocated to another former prison cell to use the glass-and-table divination technique.

Helen and I had already agreed that this room was of far greater interest to us. This was because we'd studied a lot of CCTV footage from that room when it was empty, and there were many clear signs of possible overt paranormal activity taking place there. There was an inordinate number of clear luminescent particles, or orbs, which seemed to be "intelligent" when compared to those in other rooms in the building. The infrared light was picking up dozens of these things, often in waves, with many of them changing speed, pausing in mid-air while others around them were still moving, suddenly changing both speed and trajectory, and some that even headed straight into the camera lens where they would disappear. Many of the orbs we saw on CCTV in that room fell into the annoying 5% (ish) of orbs that can't seem to be rationally explained-away and appeared to be intelligent.

Helen and I thoroughly checked that room together, and then separately, to see if there was any kind of airflow unique to that room, for excessive dust content, and for insects. There was none of the above or anything else out of the ordinary for that matter. The only thing that was different about the room was that Helen's psychic sensitivities were extremely agitated and disturbed while she was present in the room. We'd very much like to return with some scientific testing equipment to make a more detailed study of the room in terms of layout, the presence of any abnormal electromagnetic fields, geomagnetism, barometric pressure, stray radio frequencies, airflow, and air content levels, etc.

When the first team performed the glass-and-table divination technique in that room, we got what seemed to be a coherent intelligent response almost immediately. The glass-and-table divination technique is similar to operating the Ouija board. Each member of the group surrounds the table and places one finger very lightly on the rim of a down-turned glass that is on the table. Questions are then asked, and any responses are made by requested directed movement of the glass.

It seems that one person in the group who had lost a close relative was singled-out to be contacted. The glass seemed to be responding directly in an intelligent and knowledgeable way to very specific questions. This could be because contact had been made with the "spirit" of the deceased relative, alternatively, it could be some kind of subconscious response by one or more members of the group. It could also be a malevolent energy entity who was able to "hack" into their thoughts to produce a relevant response. Due to recent scientific discoveries, we now believe that this type of brain/thought "hacking" is quite possible. In this case, we simply do not know for certain what the answer is, but the session still yielded some very remarkable and interesting data.

Bodmin Jail certainly seems to be one of the most highly active places we've ever investigated and is well worth more than one visit. As well as being a fascinating place to visit from a historical perspective, it has a team of extremely talented and knowledgeable people on-hand to guide you through anything from a fascinating tour through its grizzly history, a thrilling ghost walk, or a full-scale paranormal investigation. From our own experiences there, we can honestly say that we believe that Bodmin Jail is one of the most paranormally active places in Britain. Finally, in respect of further researching witchcraft, especially in the county of Cornwall, then we'd highly recommend reading some of the excellent books by Jason Semmens.

In the United States, there are certain abandoned prison facilities which have their own places of execution. If stress and emotional energy can be absorbed into the fabric of a location, then it will certainly be found in these places. Let's face it, it doesn't get much more stressful and emotional than waiting in a jail cell overnight, knowing that the next day you'll be executed. I'd say that for anyone, that's just about as stressful and emotion-filled that any day can get. Therefore, if the theories about residual energy, stone tape recordings, and lost souls are correct, then these places will yield some excellent results. The United States is rich in abandoned prison facilities that have now become attractions for tourists and paranormal investigators. From personal experience, I'd highly recommend the West Virginia State Penitentiary built in 1876 which is a gothic-style prison in Moundsville, West Virginia. The Eastern State Penitentiary in Philadelphia, Pennsylvania built in 1829 is also excellent. The building style with the Barbican and Battlements are slightly reminiscent of Preston Jail in Lancashire, England. Overall, our advice would be to do some research and be prepared to travel to find some interesting places worthy of investigating.

Hospitals. These are another excellent location for any paranormal investigation. By virtue of what they're there to do and the service they perform, hospitals are typically reported to be highly paranormally active places. The activity you could expect to find in such places would include residual energy, stone tape recordings, and lost souls who died while being saved from accident trauma. It's easy to imagine that if the spirit goes on after the body is dead, then if someone was involved in a tragic accident and died in hospital while doctors were trying to save them, then they could easily be confused, trapped and still wandering the ethereal corridors and rooms.

Battlegrounds. Any battleground is naturally going to be a place of massive suffering, trauma and sudden death. Therefore, it's no great leap of the imagination to understand why they should be high on any paranormal investigators list of places to explore. In Britain, there are probably thousands of battle sites. Many of the most famous date back to the time of the Civil War which happened between 1642 and 1651. Notable paranormally active Civil War battlegrounds include The Battle of Marston Moor which took place in 1644 in North Yorkshire where over 4,000 men were killed. Other battlegrounds worthy of paranormal investigation include Battle Abbey on Senlac Hill. This was where The Battle of Hastings took place in 1066 between English King Harold and the invading of William of Normandy. The Battle to Towton in North Yorkshire in 1461 during the War of the Roses where approximately 30,000 people died. The Battle of Culloden in 1746 which quashed the Jacobite Rebellion. This was the defeat of the Scottish clans and the troops of Bonnie Princes Charlie. Remember the world-famous Scottish lament, The Skye Boat Song? The World War 1 Battle of Passchendaele in Belgium in 1917. British, Canadian, New Zealand, South African and Australian forces attacked the German lines and nearly 400,000 would die on both sides.

The Battle of Little Bighorn which is also known as being "Custer's Last Stand" in 1876. There the U.S. 7th Calvary was overwhelmed and defeated losing about 260 men, and the area where it happened is said to be highly active. The Battle of Gettysburg in 1863 is perhaps the bloodiest battle of the American Civil War with more than 50,000 men killed, wounded, or lost in action. The Battle of Birch Coulee Minnesota during the Dakota War of 1862 with only 13 killed and 47 wounded wasn't the bloodiest of battles in history. However, it certainly left behind a highly paranormally active location. I've investigated there on several occasions and we've never been disappointed.

These are just a small selection of the famous battle sites which can be investigated paranormally. Remember that just because a battle site might not be especially bloody when compare to others, don't rule them out. It's not always about how "blood-soaked" the ground was, or how many people died a horrible death. There are many other factors to take into consideration as to why a place might be highly paranormally active.

Orphanages. These are good locations to investigate, probably due to some of the extreme emotional distress experienced by the abandoned children. I investigated The Minnesota State Public School Orphanage Museum built in 1886 and found some extraordinary activity that was taking place. With over 10,000 children living there over and a 60-year history, this isn't very surprising. While there, I was fortunate enough to be able to interview Harvey Ronglien who was a former orphan who lived there as a child. Harvey is an amazing man and he gave me a great insight into what life was like there through the eyes of a small child in the early 20th century. I'd highly recommend investigating there and reading Harvey's book,

"A Boy from C-11 Case #9164, A Memoir" by Harvey Ronglien.

Theatres. Since a great deal of emotion is expressed during theatrical performances, it should come of no great surprise to learn that theatres are often paranormally active locations. Whether it be residual energy, the stone tape recording theory, or a combination of both or more, I know many paranormal professionals who have had great successes in theatre-centred investigations. I remember gathering some excellent evidence with a team from The International Paranormal Society while investigating the Sheldon Theatre in Red Wing, Minnesota, in the United States. The theatre was built in 1904, so by British and European standards, it's not that old. I was with a team seated on the stage performing a silent vigil for about 20 minutes for an EVP session.

Later, when we met up with the team who were in the under-stage area to compare notes, they asked us why we made so much noise. We enquired what noise they were specifically referring to. They then explained that for almost the entire time of the vigil they were surprised to hear our heavy repeated footsteps and to hear us dragging chairs and furniture about on the stage above them. The team I was with included Adrian Lee, and we just looked at each other in a knowing way without saying a word.

The other team members were shocked to learn that not one of our team members had moved or spoken a word during the entire time of the vigil after they had left us there on the stage. The playback of our EVP recordings proved that what we had said was true. The recordings also revealed the strange faint sound of footsteps and furniture being dragged around the stage area, that we couldn't hear while we were sat there in person in complete darkness.

Therefore, I'd highly recommend that you seek out old theatres that will kindly allow you access to investigate. You never know, if they're producing a good old-fashioned ghost story play then a real paranormal investigation might be exactly the sort of extra publicity they're looking for!

Restaurants. Oddly enough, restaurants can also prove fruitful in yielding evidence of paranormal activity taking place. The old ones are especially good, and the bonus of those places is that you'll probably meet there with your team prior to the investigation to eat while coordinating your plans. Forepaugh's (pronounced 'four paws') restaurant in St. Paul, Minnesota is in a building that dates to 1870 and is highly paranormally active. Many professionals who have independently investigated there concur in that conclusion. Many of the old roadhouses have some interesting activity and are worthy of exploring.

Pubs, Bars and Taverns. There are dozens of British pubs which are reputed to be haunted, many of which have some excellent CCTV footage to back this up. I've investigated one such pub several times, which is The Old Mill House Hotel in Polperro, Cornwall, England. The village of Polperro is straight out of the movie set of the fantastic "Poldark" TV series. Most houses there being several hundred years old, and some much older. The streets between them reflect their age, and some are not even wide enough to get even a small car through.

Brian Morgan is the former mayor of Polperro and the Landlord. Brian and his wife Rita first invited my wife and me to investigate the mystery of flying glasses on the bar. Thanks to Brian and Rita I now have excellent quality CCTV footage which clearly shows this phenomenon taking place. Brian is standing at the end of the bar where he is cleaning the glasses and pump nozzles towards the end of the evening. Suddenly, the CCTV clearly shows one of the glasses which is positioned on the bar in front of him being pushed by an unseen hand, right at him.

The Old Mill House Pub and Hotel, Polperro, Cornwall, England.

I deliberately used the word "pushed" because that's exactly what the CCTV shows, it didn't simply tip off the counter. Other high-quality CCTV footage of the bar which was taken overnight, and clearly shows some strange things happening at the same end of the bar. Numerous orbs can be seen in the videos, and in other videos, glasses fly across the room off the bar to land on the floor. So far, I've not been able to make contact with anything to identify who or what might be the cause of the disturbances. There is another excellent CCTV screenshot I use in my live seminars at conventions about paranormal investigating. This is a picture of it below which clearly shows a distinct shadow figure standing right next to the bar.

A CCTV screen grab caught overnight of the bar at The Old Mill House Pub. Note the shadow figure.

Another time, Rita Morgan together with my wife Helen and I, investigated some of the guest rooms in the hotel area above the bar. We were extremely surprised to get so much excellent EMF activity in direct response to our questions. We also captured several very interesting EVP's, but most of what was clearly said in the recordings didn't directly connect to our questions. It was almost as if we were listening in on another conversation in another dimension. So, more investigation will be needed,

Brian and Rita Morgan told us about the disaster which happened in 1976 and which may be the cause, at least in part, of the paranormal activity that is taking place at The Old Mill House Inn. There was a huge flood in 1976 before the modern floodwater bypass tunnel was built, and it swept away large parts of the village causing massive damage. Sadly, the then owner of The Old Mill House was also killed. Apparently, during the height of the flood, the water level rose so rapidly that he became trapped in the bar area and was swept away to his death from there. The couple who owned The Old Mill House at the time had a friend staying from London, and she also became trapped in the flood.

A close-up of the shadow figure caught on a CCTV screen grab caught overnight of the bar at The Old Mill House Pub and Hotel in Polperro, Cornwall.

Apparently, she was almost killed when trying to escape the raging flood waters which were sweeping through the ground floor bar area of the building. Fortunately, she just escaped in the nick of time, and both the landlady and her friend were saved by eventually climbing high enough to the uppermost floors of the building. When the floodwaters eventually subsided, and the village began to grasp at regaining some semblance of normality once again, the friend of the owner's wife eventually left to return home to London.

She never made it back though. As she was leaving Cornwall, the vehicle she was travelling in was involved in a crash and she was killed. It was almost as if she had been meant to die in the floodwaters sweeping through The Old Mill House Inn, but for some reason escaped her death at the time. However, death returned to reclaim her before she left Cornwall completely.

In Polperro, there is an even older building which is now a pub called The Noughts and Crosses and is about 400 to 500 years old. Lorraine Parkington was the landlady at the time, and she had frequently invited us to investigate the building. This is because both she and several members of her staff had frequently reported unusual happenings. So, we did exactly that and investigated in January 2018.

Several of the people who service the guest bedrooms had independently complained about feelings of being watched and even seeing a shadow figure in the rooms and corridors. A member of the room servicing team had also reported that the guest towels she had neatly laid out at the foot of the bed had often been moved. Occasionally, if she left the room to fetch something, then when she returned the towels had been moved to lay on the pillows. There was simply no explanation for this happening because the hotel section is very small, and every time it had happened, she knew that all the guests were already out for the day. One time she asked a colleague to service the room with her. They then left the room and locked it to take a 15-minute tea break in one of the rooms a little further down the corridor. This way they could be certain that no one could have slipped past them to move the towels in that room. After the tea break, they both returned to the room in question, and with a certain degree of trepidation, they both went inside. Sure enough, the towels had been moved from the foot of the bed where they had both placed them 15 minutes earlier and now the towels were resting on the pillows at the top of the bed.

The Noughts and Crosses Pub and Hotel, Polperro, Cornwall, England.

We decided that room 3 with the unusual towel-moving activity was probably the best place to start. So, we set up a laser grid, and EVP monitoring device, an Ovilus, a ghost box, and a trusty digital recorder to capture any potential evidence during our EVP sessions. Lorraine and the person from the room servicing team who had most frequently experienced the phenomenon were also in attendance that night.

I began the investigation by asking aloud about why whatever or whoever was there would deliberately move the towels after they'd been placed in a neat decorative style at the foot of guest's beds. Very soon into the investigation, we got our answer. A good quality EVP, together with substantiating words spoken aloud on the Ovilus and accompanied by text on the screen, suggested that the towels were indeed being moved by ghostly hands. The voice on the EVP and Ovilus replied to one of my questions by saying literally "The maid is fussy." Lorraine and her friend just sat there in silence, stunned by what they had just heard on the playback of this recording.

As the investigation continued, we asked the spirit we were apparently communicating with how old they were and where they came from. We were told that we were communicating with someone who had once lived in Polperro and worked in that building about 150 years ago, in the mid to late 19th century. They attempted to give a name several times, but it never came through clearly enough on either the Ovilus, the ghost box, or the EVP. No text of a name was ever displayed either. We then asked if there were any other spirits with them, and if so, how many there were. Almost immediately, we received a reply which shocked everyone present. We captured an EVP on all recording devices, and also in text format on the Ovilus screen as well, the words, "About 50".

These two pubs/hotels in the tiny fishing village of Polperro both proved to be extraordinary in terms of the paranormal activity we captured. My wife and I believe that many other places in the village will prove to be paranormal active too, and we should spend some time there to investigate the village in a wider sense. We're especially looking forward to returning to Polperro to stay with our friends Brian and Rita Morgan at The Old Mill House Hotel. Another time we'll be sure to stay with our other friend Lorraine Parkington at The Noughts and Crosses Pub. Both places are worthy of a much more thorough investigation, preferably outside the tourist season. We're hoping to coordinate this with fellow Brit, Adrian Lee of The International Paranormal Society so we can deploy bigger teams of experienced professionals together with a wider range of equipment. You'll read and see more about the conclusion to this story both online and in other books when the investigations have been completed.

Moving across the Atlantic in my next example, my friend Jesse Medina owns the Cadillac Bar on Flores Street in San Antonio, Texas. At only 130 years old, this limestone-built bar is an excellent example of a comparatively new building, especially when compared to the ones in Polperro, England. However, it is highly paranormally active and well worth investigating. Jesse, members of his bar team, and also many customers have all reported seeing a strange woman who simply "disappears" into the ether. Glasses have been discovered broken on the floor where none were the night before, and things seem to mysteriously move around the building. This one is still on my "to do" list, and

I'm really looking forward to seeing Jesse again to investigate there with an experienced team.

As a footnote, San Antonio, in general, has many other places that are well worth investigating. I was once walking past the Alamo and since my wife and I just happened to have an Ovilus with us, we decided to try our luck. Within seconds of asking if there was anyone or anything there, a voice replied saying "Killed", "Trauma", "Death". This would suggest they we'd successfully made contact with someone who had been killed during the world-famous siege of the Alamo in 1836.

These are just a few examples of how pubs, bars, and taverns can be highly paranormally active and yield some excellent results when investigated. I'm also fairly certain that if you look around and research some of the places in the area near to where you live, then you'll find at least one which seems to have experienced paranormal activity and would welcome an investigation. The biggest drawback to overcome is probably always going to be the reticence many people have when it comes to talking about them experiencing potential paranormal activity. I usually find that once people have overcome their initial reticence, then they generally "open-up" freely about events that might be worthy of investigating.

Ships and boats. It is surprising just how many ships and boats seem to be haunted, especially by those who have died on them from a traumatic accident. The Steam Ship William A. Irvin is one such ship. It is a 610-foot-long, 13,000-ton ore freighter on Great Lakes of the United States and Canada. The ship has now been restored and permanently moored in Duluth, Minnesota, on Lake Superior. During the ship's career, there were many unfortunate accidents aboard, and one proved fatal for the victim, William Wuori aged 59 who was scalded to death by escaping steam in a boiler room accident. William Wuori's ghost has been frequently witnessed by many people since that time as it wanders around the ship. The ship is has become so well-known for the paranormal activity taking place on broad that the owners operate regular ghost tours for the public. By special arrangement, they will also allow professional paranormal investigation.

More importantly, thanks to the paranormal author and historian Adrian Lee's research, we now know that William Wuori is directly related to my wife, Helen Renee Wuorio. Apparently, William Wuori was her Great Uncle. Adrian's research found out that in those days, it was very common for people in families of immigrants from places like Finland to simply drop awkward letters from their name to make it easier to pronounce and write in their new country. This is exactly what William Wuori did, and it is also why it required Adrian's extensive research to uncover the truth of the matter. The SS William A. Irvin is an excellent example of a paranormally active ship which can be investigated. This is definitely at the top of our "places to investigate" list when we next return to Duluth, Minnesota.

Interestingly, there's a paranormal twist which would make anyone think twice about doubting if some people are genuinely gifted with psychic ability. During the summer of 2018, my wife and I were visiting Duluth,

Minnesota with close family friends from Manchester, England. As we were all approaching the bow of the SS Willian A. Irvin, my mobile phone rang. The call was from Adrian Lee, who is a renowned psychic. After we greet each other briefly and catch up, Adrian proceeds to tell me that his publisher wants a specific picture for the front cover shot for his latest book, "Mysterious Minnesota: Digging Up the Ghostly Past at Thirteen Haunted Sites".

Adrian was calling for a special reason. Since my wife Helen and I were in Minnesota, he was wondering if we would like to join him as he travelled to take a few pictures of either Fort Snelling or the SS Willian A. Irvin for the book cover. As he was explaining this to me over the phone, Adrian suddenly stopped speaking, and the line went silent. After a few seconds, he then said to me, "Something's telling me to ask you... oh, it's the SS Willian A. Irvin, why is something telling me to ask you about this ship right now?"

The SS William A. Irvin Moored on Lake Superior in Duluth, Minnesota, USA.

Initially, I was dumbstruck, and couldn't find the right words in my head to reply to what Adrian had just said. I then proceeded to tell Adrian that at the very moment when he called me on the phone, I was stood right at the front of the SS Willian A. Irvin in Duluth. Furthermore, I had literally just taken several good pictures of the ship on a high-resolution mobile phone camera. The very ship that "something" had just compelled him to ask me about. I then asked him if he wanted me to email them to him to see if they would work for the new book cover. I did, and they were EXACTLY what was envisioned. Therefore, the picture of the SS Willian A. Irvin on the front cover of Adrian Lee's book "Mysterious Minnesota: Digging Up the Ghostly Past at Thirteen Haunted Sites" has a paranormal connection. Adrian's amazing psychic abilities enabled him to somehow "know" where I was and what I was doing, which is why this picture was used on the book cover. This entire episode was witnessed by our previously sceptical British friends. After this incident, and especially after meeting Adrian in person, they returned home as firm believers in the existence of psychic powers, and Adrian Lee's amazing abilities!

The SS William A. Irvin on Adrian's Book Cover

Adrian's book, "Mysterious Minnesota: Digging Up the Ghostly Past at Thirteen Haunted Sites" is a fascinating and informative read. Adrian's abilities as a paranormal investigator, a forensic historian, and as an author are unparalleled, and I highly recommend this, and all the other books he has written. You can find Adrian's books on Amazon and through Calumet Editions. You can link with him on Facebook and also find the links to his hilarious weekly paranormal radio show, "More Questions Than Answers" (MQTA) which is broadcast worldwide on Dark Matter Digital Radio and then archived on Soundcloud.

The comparison of The SS William A. Irvin as it was moored as the picture was taken at the same time Adrian Lee was making the psychic link phone call to me, and the resultant cover for his new book.

Old Mansions, Castles and Stately Homes.

Unfortunately for those of you who live in the United States and Canada, there aren't many of these places in your respective countries compared to Britain and Europe. If you live in either the United States and Canada, then you must dig a little deeper into your research to find similar types of buildings that fit the bill and that are potentially paranormally active. I'm confident that you'll find several if you do your research. Even though they won't be very old in world terms it still doesn't mean that they aren't highly paranormally active. You simply don't know until you explore them, and as we all know, you often find paranormal activity where you least expect to find it.

In the United States and Canada many of the large older buildings that have become hotels in more recent times. This means that even if you can't get official permission to investigate the building as a whole, you can usually book an overnight stay for you and your team in the rooms with most haunted reputations.

In respect of castles, there are a few. However, they're not castles in the British or European sense of the word. Many of these "castles" are now hotels, so just like with the large older mansion house style of buildings, you can almost certainly book an overnight stay. If not, then some of them have daily tours you can join. You may not be able to deploy a wide range of fixed equipment for a thorough investigation, but you can easily carry an Ovilus, a Mel Meter, a camera, and an EMF meter with you.

To get you started, here's a short list of a few of the larger older buildings and houses with a reputation for paranormal activity in the United States and Canada.

- The Whaley House, San Diego, California
- Villisca Axe Murder House, Villisca, Iowa

- Lizzie Borden House, Fall River, Massachusetts
- The Pirate's House, Savannah, Georgia
- Robinson Rose House, San Diego, California
- The Octagon House, Washington D.C.
- The Fairlawn Mansion, Wisconsin
- The Glensheen Mansion, Minnesota
- Ottawa Jail Hostel, Ontario
- Craigdarroch Castle, British Columbia
- Banff Springs Hotel, Alberta
- Royal York Hotel, Ontario

Here's a list of the even fewer buildings that resemble "castles" that are in the United States and Canada.

- Hearst Castle, California
- Fonthill Castle, Pennsylvania
- Biltmore Estate, North Carolina
- Castello di Amorosa, California
- Boldt Castle, New York
- Thornewood Castle, Washington
- Bannerman Castle, New York
- Dundurn Castle, Hamilton, Ontario
- Craigdarroch Castle, Victoria, British Columbia
- Hatley Park Castle, Colwood, British Columbia
- Castle Loma, Toronto, Ontario

If you know of a large abandoned derelict old house/building that might be worth investigating, then start by contacting the owners. This process can sometimes be painstakingly long and tedious, so don't hold your breath and expect a quick answer to your enquiries. However, you never know for sure until you try, so be polite and be persistent. Remember, the answer is always no if you don't even ask.

In Britain and Europe, there are so many stately homes, mansions and castles that I won't even compile a short list for you. If you want to find any of these then the internet is the place to look. There are lists of them galore if you type in a simple search for them. From personal experience, some of the most active locations that we've investigated are Urquhart Castle on the banks of Loch Ness in Scotland, Conwy Castle in North Wales, St. Michael's Mount in Cornwall, and Lilford Hall in Northamptonshire.

Urquhart Castle, Loch Ness, Scotland.

When we were visiting Loch Ness in Scotland, it was natural to visit Urquhart Castle which literally sits right next to the water of the loch. The castle you see today dates back to the 13th, but it was built over the site of a much early medieval fortification. Therefore, people have been living, loving, laughing, crying and dying there in battles for well over a thousand years. So, it shouldn't be very surprising to learn that the entire area of the castle and the grounds gave readings that suggested paranormal activity was pretty widespread there.

Urquhart Castle, Loch Ness, Scotland.

We weren't on an official investigation when we first visited, so Helen and I only carried with us a Mel Meter, an Ovilus and a stills camera. But this was more than enough equipment to gather some interesting readings. The most active places we found were in the old food storage area near the entrance to the castle, the old keep, and the structures around it. When we were in the old food storage area the words we recorded in response to our questions were uncannily accurate to the location we were in. Overall, they appeared to be intelligent responses.

The drawbridge area was active too. The tourist centre, the film shows about the history of the castle, and snack bar/restaurant are some of the very best we've experienced anywhere, and they're highly recommended. Since our first visit, we've been involved in trying to arrange a formal overnight investigation with a team. To date, we've not completed this so the full report will be in another publication at a later date when we hopefully have something interesting to report.

Conwy Castle, Wales.

Conwy Castle proved to be very similar to Urquhart Castle. It's definitely paranormally active and even a tour around it with limited equipment will yield some interesting results. Just like with Urquhart Castle, once inside you're allowed to go virtually everywhere that's deemed to be safe which was part of the old castle structure. It's not a small place, and the ground can be a little uneven in places so be prepared for that. You also need to be prepared to climb the steep pathway up to the castle, and once you're inside you'll need to negotiate several small winding stone staircases to the upper battlements etc. Conwy Castle was built by King Edward I between 1283 and 1289, so there's plenty of history to it.

The most interesting readings we got during several visits to the castle were always around the old feasting hall. The basement areas, and especially the old dungeon area was also very interesting. Each time we visited we'd receive several interesting words over the Ovilus which always corresponded to where we were in the castle. The Mel Meter and EMF reader supported the suggestion that there was paranormal activity there during our Ovilus sessions.

St. Michael's Mount in Cornwall

St Michael's Mount was the Cornish counterpart of Mont Saint-Michel in Normandy, France, and it has been privately owned by St. Aubyn family since approximately 1650. Archaeologists have revealed that the island has had buildings on it where people have lived since the Neolithic period, from around 4,000 to 2,500 years BC. Therefore, this place was once a part of some very old civilisations, and there have been people living there for thousands of years. Perhaps this is why there have been such a wide variety of hauntings that have been reported to take place there.

St. Michael's Mount in Cornwall was a real surprise for us because many of the official guides were only too happy to talk about the alleged hauntings. Some of them were even keen paranormal enthusiasts, and they kindly took us into some of the private areas of the castle to take readings. One gentleman in particular who worked there told us about the many residual hauntings that seem to take place there. One of the best apparently takes place occasionally in the old picture gallery corridor towards the centre of the main structure. Once again, we have only been lightly "armed" during our several visits to date, with only a Mel Meter, and Ovilus, a stills camera and an EMF reader. There was a lot of activity we found in and around the entranceway hall, and also in the old picture gallery corridor as predicted. As well as residual hauntings that take place there, we gathered evidence to suggest there is at least one intelligent haunting.

Two very interesting responses we got were collected on a mobile phone app which we don't usually use very much because we prefer to use dedicated devices. It was via a simple Ovilus app. We'd only switched it on as a backup device, but when we passed by the main fireplace the text and voice said, "coal", and then when we passed by a spectacularly framed picture, the device said, "frame".

Perhaps the most unusual paranormally active location that I've investigated to date, was Lilford Hall in Northamptonshire, England. The core of the old building dates back late in 1495, and the more modern sections were built in 1632. This was the home of Robert Browne and his family. He is the man who taught the Pilgrim Fathers their values and persuaded them to get on board the Mayflower and seek a new life by settling Plymouth Colony in America in 1620. Therefore, Robert Browne is the man who could genuinely be called "The Grandfather of the United States".

Lilford Hall, Northamptonshire, England.

I stayed at this place for a total of 10 months from 2013 to 2013 while I produced a TV documentary about Robert Browne and Lilford Hall. This has since been shown on several channels around the world and on some PBS channels in the United States. In order to produce the TV documentary, I gathered a team of 12 people together to stay there with me. These were all seasoned TV crew, and none were especially interested in anything paranormal.

During our first week staying there in November of 2012, my team were alone and preparing our camping equipment to bed down for the night. Therefore, to prevent drafts we decided to ensure that all windows were closed in the 110 rooms there are in the building. Since the place is huge, we decided to do this together as a group before we went out to a local restaurant for our evening meal. We began in the old basement kitchen area in the North Wing of the building and work our way up and around from there until the job was done. As we did so we also decided that for the sake of security we would close and lock, or bolt, all the doors behind us. Once we'd done this, we then locked the front door behind us and went out to eat. When we returned we were in for a big surprise.

Not long after we had walked back into the building again, we noticed that one of the doors we had all witnessed being locked with an old rusty bolt earlier was now wide open. This prompted us to investigate further and retrace the steps we took earlier as a group when we'd all locked up. All the doors we had locked only a couple hours earlier were now wide open. We then relocked each one methodically while sticking together as a group. In the half hour that it took us to walk around the house, by the time we'd returned to the starting point, the doors were all open again. There was no logical explanation for this. This triggered a whole series of baffling paranormal activity which plagued us for the entire 10 months we were there. We even brought in one of our experienced teams to help us investigate, and they were mystified too. We're now planning a major investigation which will be the subject of an entire TV show I'll produce and an accompanying book.

Chapter 6: The Different Types of Hauntings

An Intelligent Haunting. Hauntings can be broken down according to type, and no two will be exactly the same. There are a variety of reasons why an entity/spirit might remain in and around one location. So, to begin with I'll outline what paranormal professionals call an "intelligent" haunting.

A haunting is considered to be "intelligent" when the entity is aware of living humans and can interact with them in various ways. For all intents and purposes, the entity seems to be able to reason, think, act, feel, and respond to human beings. The entity is also aware of the surroundings where it "resides".

If, as it would typically seem, these entities were once human, then remember that they were once just as alive as you are. Therefore, they once shared all the same hopes, dreams, fears, love, and emotions that you experience. Therefore, be respectful. You'd not meet another person in your daily life and immediately be aggressive or disrespectful towards them, so never behave that way to a spirit or any other paranormal entity.

In life, some people are nice, warm, genial, and friendly. Therefore, in death, their spirit will possess the same qualities. Whereas some people in life are nasty, irritable, criminal and down-right evil, and in death, their spirit will probably be the same as it was in life. Again, in life, there are the jokers and mischief-makers, and in death, their spirit will retain the same qualities they had in life.

Naturally, the spirits of angry, criminal and evil people will prove to be just as dangerous in death as they were in life. Although they might not be a "demon", they are the entities that will cause as much harm to the living as they possibly can. These are the ones that will push you downstairs, scratch you, and throw debris at you, etc. Therefore, beware of them, and never underestimate them. It's also worth remembering that investigators often injure themselves far more when they panic and run through fear, as opposed to injuries inflicted by the spirit/entity itself.

In an intelligent haunting, objects will move, doors will open, knocking noises will be heard, and drafts felt. It's worth considering that entities might be seeking nothing more than your attention because they're lonely or want to pass a message onto you for some reason.

Unfinished Business Hauntings. There is a theory that some spirits haunt a location due to some sort of "unfinished business" they believe they must still complete. This type of intelligent haunting usually occurs when physical death has been caused suddenly, often as the result of an accident of some sort. In this scenario, the spirit is locked in some sort of "shock" due to the trauma which killed them physically.

They seem to remain to haunt the location until they either believe that the unfinished business has been completed, of they've been "helped" to move on in some way. If they wish to move on, and a medium helps them to do so, then the process is usually facilitated by the medium discovering what the unfinished business is that the spirit believes it must complete.

Hauntings to Help People. These are linked to how some spirits believing they still have unfinished business they need to complete in our realm. Some spirits believe that they need to remain and help a loved one or family member in some way. Many people report this type of haunting occurred during a particularly troubling time in their life, and the spirit of the deceased loved one was returning to help them.

This type of haunting often includes certain odours being reported which were related to the spirit when they were alive. This could include a certain type of tobacco smoke, or a particular brand of perfume, etc.

Hauntings to Say Goodbye. It seems that some intelligent hauntings occur because the spirit feels the need to say goodbye to loved ones and friends before moving on. Again, this is related to the "unfinished business" type of haunting. This category of haunting is usually short in overall duration and are either through a physical apparition complete with interaction or as part of someone's exceptionally vivid dream.

An excellent example of this sort of haunting where the spirit of the deceased needed to say "goodbye", together with a demonstration of quantum bilocation and a nonlinear time-space anomaly happened during World War 1 at Castle Leslie in Ireland. The castle already had long been reputed as a highly paranormally active location, and it is apparently still haunted by several ghosts to this day.

Norman Leslie was the second son of Colonel Sir John Leslie, of Castle Leslie, in County Monaghan, Ireland. Interestingly, his mother was the sister of Sir Winston Churchill's mother, Jennie. On October the 18th in 1914 Norman Leslie was killed whilst leading a charge against a German machine gun, while armed with only his sword. The juxtaposition of sword vs. machine gun concept always baffles me though.

Incredibly, Normal Leslie was seen by several estate workers both on the castle terrace and walking around the gardens a full week *before* he was killed in action. At the time he was seen, the Leslie family were overjoyed when several estate workers reported seeing Norman at home again. Naturally, they thought that he must have been on leave from the army and paid them a surprise visit. However, their joy quickly turned to extreme anxiety when he failed to be at dinner that evening. Naturally, this prompted a search of the house and estate to try and find him. It was to no avail, he was never found because he had never returned home and was still fighting on the Western Front with his regiment. The family even made official enquires about his whereabouts, and it was confirmed that he'd never left the continent.

About a week later, a telegram arrived at Castle Leslie reporting the death of Colonel Leslie at the Battle of Armentieres, several days *after* he was seen by several people back at the castle. No explanation could be found as to how the future ghost of Norman Leslie could be seen back at the castle before he had even died.

I believe that this remains one of the most interesting and baffling examples of the spirit of the deceased needed to say “goodbye”. Since we can safely assume that the many independent eyewitnesses to this phenomenon were all reliable, and hadn’t conspired to conceive an incredible hoax, then there can only be one possible explanation. This is that bilocation is possible through some form of quantum entanglement, that time is indeed nonlinear, and that time travel is also possible.

Confused Hauntings. Some spirits seem to be completely confused. They have no idea that they are physically dead and now only exist in spirit form. This type of intelligent haunting is common when death has been very sudden, usually as the result of an accident.

Trapped hauntings. In some hauntings, the spirit seems to be “trapped” in some way. Typically, with this type of haunting, the spirit is aware of both surroundings and the living people it intelligently interacts with, and this is why it falls under the category of being an “intelligent” haunting. Almost always, the spirt will have some sort of strong connection to either the place it haunts and/or the people who live or work there.

Fear Hauntings. Fear of something also seems to be another reason why an intelligent haunting might occur. The fear might be caused by almost anything, even because they fear moving-on for some reason. It’s possible that they might fear whatever awaits them in the next phase of their existence. The fact is that we simply don't know.

Random Hauntings. Some hauntings seem to be completely random in nature, such as when a spirit returns to visit a friend or loved one. They can happen at a time of danger or crisis, or during a happy event such as a wedding or birth. Whatever the reason, this type of haunting is usually brief and for a specific purpose. Therefore, it's not really a "haunting" in the classical sense of the word.

Residual Hauntings. A residual haunting is very different from an intelligent haunting. With a residual haunting, there is no intelligent interaction with anyone who witnesses it. It's almost always as though those witnessing it are looking at a video playback of something.

Therefore, this type of haunting is connected to the "Stone Tape Theory". This is that all types of physical objects such as stone, wood and metal can absorb energy and record events, especially those that are highly emotionally charged. It is also connected with the replay of events which can apparently be stored in objects such as pictures, mirrors, and vases, etc.

This could also at least partially explain why over the centuries countless "residual" apparitions have been reported of entire villages, towns, armies, and ships being seen for a brief period of time and often in an unexpected location. This is a little like the concept of the mythical "Brigadoon", where the village only appears once every 100 years in the mists of the Scottish Highlands.

Angel Hauntings. Angelic hauntings are extremely rare and very unusual in nature. Most reported angelic hauntings and/or apparitions tend to be when someone is experiencing an extreme crisis or even a near-death experience. Even though we don't know precisely what they are, it's perfectly possible that an angel could come to aid a human being in this sort of scenario. There again, it's equally possible that such an apparition could simply be a stress-induced hallucination. The fact is that we simply don't know for certain. Whatever the reason, people who witness angels under these circumstances often dramatically change their life and lifestyle as a result, and they also typically become deeply religious afterwards.

Demonic Hauntings. Like angelic hauntings, there are also demonic hauntings. Demonic hauntings aren't really a haunting in the typical sense of the word, instead, they're a form of possession. Demons are an extremely malevolent form of negative paranormal entity which has enormous energy and extensive powers. Since it is believed that for a demon to enter our realm they must be invited in somehow, the best way to prevent them is by not inviting anything in which might be harmful. This is like how hyperlinks in seemingly benign junk email might be infected with an extremely harmful virus that can severely damage your computer once you have invited it in by opening the "benign" email. Like angels, demons could be either purely an energy-based paranormal entity of some sort, or possibly even some kind of badly observed extraterrestrial beings who don't like humans very much. The bottoms line is that we simply don't really know precisely what they are, but what we do know is that they are extremely dangerous.

Poltergeist Hauntings. Poltergeist haunting isn't strictly a haunting. They mostly consist of physical disturbances such as knocking noises, objects being moved, and objects being thrown. They can even move heavy objects and there have been many recorded incidents of people being physically levitated and thrown, and other kinds of physical attack resulting in injury to those involved.

We know that Poltergeist activity almost always centres on and around a certain person known as the "epicentre" of the activity. However, we also know that poltergeist activity is certainly not confined to being centred on and around teenage girls as it was once thought. When an older person is the epicentre of an outbreak it is believed to be caused due to extreme stress and often the activation of certain previously repressed memories which triggers their latent and uncontrolled telekinetic abilities. This is why some scientists believe that poltergeist activity has nothing to do with a paranormal entity.

Alternatively, some people believe that a poltergeist is nothing to do with people causing the activity through the activation of latent powers. Instead, they believe it involves some type of purely paranormal energy entity which "feeds" on the emotional energy being generated by whoever is at the epicentre of the activity.

Whatever the cause, poltergeist activity usually seems to be intelligent in nature, and an outbreak can last from as little as a few weeks to several years. However, a poltergeist outbreak is usually very short in duration, with events ceasing as mysteriously as they suddenly began.

Chapter 7: What Not to do When Paranormal Investigating

First and foremost, DO NOT TRESPASS! When investigating any location, no matter how abandoned, isolated or remote it might look, always take the trouble to seek official permission first. This should preferably be in writing, and it's always a good idea for each team member to have a printed copy of the permission that has been granted to your team. If you don't gain proper permission, then you could end up in a great deal of trouble. You could face arrest, criminal prosecution, private prosecution, damaging media coverage, and a criminal record.

Being respectful of another person's property is essential. In addition, you should always respect whatever entities you communicate with. Failure to adhere to any of these rules will not only give you a bad name, but it will also undermine the respectability and status of all paranormal investigators. If you develop a reputation for having a cavalier attitude to respect for property and entities, then very soon you'll find that you and your team aren't welcome anywhere. When investigating, or even when simply visiting cemetery's, battlefields and anywhere where someone has died, then please be particularly respectful.

Never investigate anywhere alone. To do so makes no sense. if you investigate alone it isn't showing how brave you are for being in a "haunted" location. Instead, it simply shows anyone with any intelligence that you're not reputable and professional.

More importantly, any evidence that you might gather during a solo investigation is invalid and technically non-admissible. This is because there is only your word that it isn't fake, and your credibility is going to already be in doubt simply because you've investigated alone, and not as part of a team. There is simply no way to verify any of the evidence you collect. Even if it's jackpot time, and you encounter a full-body apparition, you sit down and have a chat with it while drinking a cuppa tea or coffee, you might even share a few laughs and take a few selfies of you both. The simple fact is that no one will ever really believe you!

In addition to the issue of validating the evidence, there is also the danger factor to consider. Safety is always of paramount importance and investigating alone simply brings many more unacceptable risk factors into the equation. It's just a fact that most of the places that will be investigated during a ghost hunt will be buildings that are old and abandoned. These will be fraught with dangers of all kinds. These include damaged floors, some levels having no floor at all, corridors with doors which open to a huge drop below, bits of debris, and many more unacceptable safety issues. During a paranormal investigation outdoors, there are even more potential dangers. These include fall risks, rock falls, hidden caves, sinkholes, water hazards, electrical hazards, wild animal dangers, falling trees, dangerous branches, rocks, the risk of drowning, exposure other risks, hypothermia (extreme cold) or hyperthermia (heatstroke), and many more. ALWAYS investigate as part of a team of responsible people who can be relied on to do the right thing should an emergency ever arise.

Occasionally, the presence of an entity is detected via the scent or smell of something. It can be a pleasant smell, or it can be a foul smell, or somewhere in between. Therefore, there should be a complete ban on all perfume, aftershave, strong mints being chewed, and smoking of any kind during all investigations. Any of these will contaminate the location and render the investigation null and void. Even if someone has smoked a cigarette somewhere well away from the investigation area will create a problem. This is because the scent of stale smoke on their breath will contaminate the investigation area when they return. Occasionally smoke/vapour/mist has been clearly detected in photographs taken during investigations. Therefore, any risk of contaminating your evidence just isn't worth taking.

Your sense of smell during any paranormal investigation/ghost hunt is a critical factor. This is because the sense of smell completely bypasses the thalamus. The thalamus is the brain's relay centre for all sensory signals, and almost all receptors pass signals through the thalamus first for it to pre-interpret before relaying those signals to the proper areas of the brain for perception. The sense of smell has its own olfactory bulb that directly interprets everything you smell. This is highly significant, especially during a paranormal investigation. Since this is the only sense that does not travel to the thalamus before accessing the forebrain, whatever you smell during an investigation is real, and not an illusion. This is unlike your other senses which can be fooled by the pre-interpretation centre of the thalamus, your sense of smell has a direct hotwire link to your brain. For this reason alone, it's well worth imposing a mandatory ban on smoking, perfume, and scent.

It should go without saying that during any investigation there should be no tom-foolery, horseplay, or messing around of any kind. There's a big difference between these things and genuine high spirits (no pun intended there) and enjoyment amongst team members. When the line is crossed into anything beyond that, then it isn't acceptable. Chit-chat and jokes are fine before the investigation, but they're unacceptable during the investigation itself. You might be capturing the most amazing ethereal voice recording ever, only to find that your evidence is contaminated to the point of making it useless by the chatting noises of other team members. This would be incredibly frustrating, to say the least. Always be focused on the investigation and always be professional.

Provocation of any entity you encounter or communicate with is totally unacceptable. On a ghost hunt, you're typically attempting to communicate with an energy entity. Theoretically at least, this will be the spirit of someone who was once a living human being. However, you have no guarantee of that. No matter how convincing the entity might be with whom you're communicating, you should never 100% believe that they are who they say they are. There is simply no way to verify that. Therefore, if you use provocation then you also risk the danger of attack and attachment by that entity. A physical attack may take the form of scratches, being pushed, having your hair pulled, or having debris or objects thrown at you. None of which is very pleasant. To make matters even worse, you could find that an entity attaches itself to you, which can be extremely dangerous. I'll explain more about this in the next chapter.

Chapter 8: The Dangers of Paranormal Investigating and How to Protect Yourself

There are serious dangers that may be encountered when paranormal investigating. Since ghost hunting has become increasingly popular in recent years because of the many TV shows about the subject, there are now many more inexperienced paranormal investigators than ever before. This has resulted in a dramatic rise in incidences of inexperienced investigators suffering physical injury, mental attack, attachment, and even total possession as a result.

Every religion on earth follows the belief in the existence of entities with supernatural powers of both good, and evil. If you're religious and believe in a higher power, then you're basically believing in a deity which is a supernatural energy entity committed to all things good, and which has a positive effect on you and your life. Similarly, if you believe in a higher power that is "good", then as sure as night follows day, there must also be an equal "dark" higher power to counterbalance it.

Translate this into more scientific terminology, then the good and evil become positive and negative energy. I believe that many of the more serious problems begin when people don't have total belief in whatever deity they follow. I say "whatever" deity, not to be disrespectful, but because whether you like it or not, there are many religions that people follow, and each religion believes that they are the only ones who have it right. Therefore, I'm just being respectful to all. In respect of the power of belief, to just blindly somehow believe that good will always overcome evil doesn't really cut it. Even if you were taught this many years ago when you attended some religious class as a child, it doesn't work if the 100% belief factor isn't there. However, there is another problem in blindly believing that good will automatically always somehow overcome evil. The universe doesn't work like that. NOTHING in existence in our universe is out of balance with everything else. There simply cannot be one form of energy which is stronger than another, both must be balanced in some way.

I believe that the balance of good and evil, or positive and negative, is in some way like the shape of an ever-changing metaphoric Yin-Yang, or Taijitu symbol. The Taijitu in Chinese philosophy is a symbolic depiction of how seemingly opposing forces may be complementary, interconnected, and interdependent to each other. I believe that in the real world and universe around us, one where religious beliefs and science can overlap and even complement each other, this shape is always going to be flexible, and ever-changing.

As the force of "good" with its positive energy becomes stronger in one way, it causes the force of "darkness" with its negative energy to retreat by the same amount in another area. Similarly, as the force of "darkness" retreats in one area, then the universe must counterbalance this, and cause the force of "good" to retreat correspondingly in another area. I believe that the existence of good and evil, positive and negative, light and dark, whatever you may wish to call them, must always be in some sort of balance with each other. These are basic laws of physics, and everything in the universe works according to physical laws. If it didn't, then the universe itself would simply unravel, and we would have never even existed in the first place.

Never Investigate at Home

There is a "golden rule" that you should never paranormally investigate your home, and this should never be violated. If you investigate at home, then it can inadvertently attract energy and entities that weren't there to begin with. This can bring with it a plethora of problems that are all caused by you.

A member of my own family was directly affected by a paranormal entity, and a more serious attack was thankfully thwarted in the nick of time. This happened simply because he foolishly decided to download and use a ghost hunting app on his mobile phone while at home. This person, I'll call him John for the sake of privacy, decided to try using one of the many proprietary ghost hunting apps that can be downloaded by anyone, usually for free.

The moment he turned on the application, the phone started acting crazy. It began flashing up a red screen which he'd never seen before, and the phone's speaker began emitting metallic sounding words accompanied by text on the screen which said the same thing. It gave a specific name, which was David, then it said aloud and wrote the words, "crash", "drunk", and then "killed". John told me that at the same time this was happening his two large dogs immediately ran to a certain wall in the lounge. Once there, they both constantly looked upwards at a fixed point and began incessant barking at something which was unseen to him but was obviously visible to the dogs.

Naturally, this deeply disturbed him, especially when the dogs continued to be significantly disturbed throughout that night. His wife reported the same information about the incident during a separate interview. He immediately deleted the app from his mobile phone, and since John and his wife both share the same deep religious beliefs, they prayed intensely. Thankfully, after a few days of frequent and intense prayer, everything settled back to normal again.

John then decided to investigate the name and alleged drunken crash which had flashed onto his mobile phone screen and caused the huge disruption. He was easily able to access data through the internet. He discovered on the road outside of their house, the one adjacent to the wall which the dogs had been barking at, there had been an incident some years earlier. The records showed that there had been a man called David who had been killed in a motorbike accident on that same road next to his house. The records also showed that the autopsy reported that the man had a very high level of alcohol in his blood at the time of the accident. Once it had been activated, the ghost app had apparently channelled the man called David who had been killed several years prior by being drunk while riding his motorbike. Furthermore, it had done so with great accuracy.

There's only one way to say this, and I'll emphasise it strongly again. NEVER USE GHOST HUNTING EQUIPMENT AT HOME, AND NEVER USE IT FLIPPANTLY UNDER ANY CIRCUMSTANCES ON ANY LOCATION. To do so can place you and those around you in great danger. It was only fortunate for John that he and his wife have unshakable religious beliefs, together with a support network of highly experienced paranormal experts to fall back on.

When it comes to your home, you should always be aware of certain indicators that may point to the possibility of paranormal activity taking place there. Therefore, I'd recommend that you keep a close eye on what's happening at home, especially after investigating other paranormal active locations.

This is because you never really know for certain what entities might have chosen to take up residence in your home. This is especially true if for any reason your injunctions of protection both before and after an investigation aren't powerful enough to prevent entities leaving with you as attachments. Don't forget, they may choose to lie dormant for quite some time before revealing themselves. Listen for strange noises that you've never heard before, unusual footsteps, scratching, knocking or muffled voices/whispers.

Become aware of any unusual animal-like noises and guttural, growling sounds that don't make sense, because they may not be coming from the outside or next door. If you own pets, then take note of any strange behaviour they may suddenly exhibit. Perhaps they're constantly staring at an unusual spot/location, or they refuse to walk up or downstairs. Perhaps they shake violently when you pick them up and carry them up or down those stairs. It is commonly believed that animals can see and sense entities which we're unable to as humans, so they're always an excellent indicator that something has changed in your home and is out of kilter.

Strange odours are another excellent indicator of possible paranormal activity taking place because your sense of smell is extremely reliable and can't easily be fooled. I explain more about why this is in a later chapter.

The movement, relocating of, or inexplicable disappearance of inanimate objects is another possible indicator of paranormal activity. This includes furniture, ornaments, doors, drawers and cupboards opening and closing, and lights turning on and off on their own etc. External vibrations could affect the movement of objects in your home, so don't rule this out as being the explanation.

Unusual temperature changes, and inexplicable cold, or hot spots can indicate possible paranormal activity taking place. Naturally, one should always go to great lengths to investigate and eliminate all rational explanations first before jumping to any paranormal conclusions.

Naturally, visual apparitions of something/someone are a good indicator of paranormal activity taking place. In addition, if you or a family member is physically touched by an unseen entity, or possibly pushed, have hair pulled or lifted, then these are also almost definite indicators of serious paranormal activity occurring.

If any of these things are experienced in your own home, it's important not to panic and react irrationally. Instead of reacting, one should always respond. There's a huge difference between the two. Typically, paranormal entities want to generate fear and extreme emotion. This is because some entities may feed off this fear in some way, or simply derive warped pleasure from it. Don't give them the opportunity. The calmer you remain, the better things will be.

If your home is suffering from increasingly intense paranormal activity, then call experienced professionals to help deal with it. Do not attempt to do anything about it yourself if you don't have the required experience and knowledge to deal with it properly. Alternatively, if you already have the required skills and knowledge, then you know exactly what to do, and who to call if you need help.

Physical Attacks

In respect of physical attacks, there are several ways in which you can be attacked through interaction with paranormal entities/ghosts. The most obvious being literally any kind of physical attack. This can be through something such as debris, or an object being thrown at you. Logic would indicate that the more powerful the energy entity is that you're dealing with, then the greater the mass of the object that the energy is potentially able to move. Being pushed is another possible form of physical attack that must be seriously considered, especially when standing near a high drop, or at the top of stairs/ladders. Again, the greater the energy which the entity possesses, the greater its potential ability to push harder and faster.

The most violent paranormal physical attack I ever experienced was in November of 2014. There was a house near to where I was staying at the time in Minneapolis, Minnesota in the United States which was experiencing some extremely unusual paranormal activity. There were strange noises heard, shadow figures seen in the basement, and the pet cats were obviously too scared to enter certain rooms at times, and one of them was physically attacked so violently that it screamed in pain.

I was asked to arrange a clearing of whatever negative energy had taken up residence there, which I did. The night before the clearing was due to take place the owners were away, so I volunteered to stay there to look after the animals. During the evening the house had been unusually quiet, with no perceivable paranormal activity taking place anywhere.

I went to bed at about 10 pm thinking all would be well and wore my usual track pants and sweatshirt. These were ideal clothes to wear in case I needed to jump out of bed to deal with an emergency. So, there was nothing out of the ordinary in what I was wearing. I had only been asleep for about 30 minutes, and I woke to feel the most painful burning sensation to my inner left forearm that I'd ever experienced. With the light now on, I first looked at the sleeve of my sweatshirt where I'd just experienced the burning sensation. I was mystified to see that it was soaking wet from the elbow down to my hand. Since I'd been sleeping with both of my arms on top of the bed covers, there was no explanation for this.

I then rolled back my sleeve. To my surprise, there were huge reddened blister burns covering most of my inner forearm. It was clearly raised in several huge welts, and some of them had burst which must have caused my sleeve to be wet. I immediately grabbed my mobile phone and took several pictures of it to record the incident. It was fortunate that I did take pictures, because miraculously about 45 minutes after I'd woken up to find the burn, it had completely disappeared as if it had never been there in the first place.

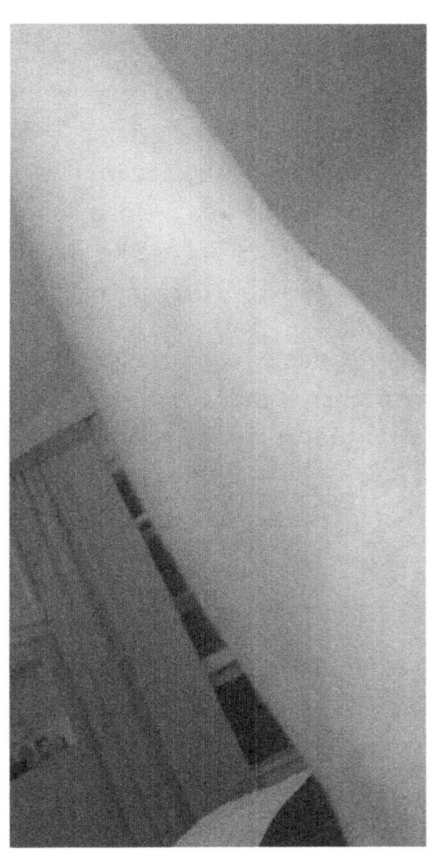

The blister burns on my arm.

I then tried to rationally explore every possible explanation why this might have happened but to no avail. I'd been wearing the same sweatshirt for several days at night in bed, so there was no possibility that it could have been caused from an allergic reaction to the washing powder I'd used to launder my clothes in. Besides, it was the same detergent I'd always used with no problems before or since that time. I wasn't allergic to the cats, and they hadn't even been near me that evening anyway, so it wasn't them. I'd not sleepwalked and held my arm against anything hot. Lastly, the roof wasn't leaking, and no pipes had burst in the room either. There was simply no rational explanation of what and how this could have happened any other way except paranormally.

I believe that whatever entity had taken up residence at the house was sentient. It knew that I had arranged for it to be evicted the next day and it was very angry at me. Which was why it attacked me by burning me during my overnight stay. As you might imagine, this unprovoked attack prompted me to take deliberate action.

I proceeded to go all around the house, starting in the basement and working my way upstairs while stating aloud clear words of protection. I commanded the thing in the most definite words, that under no circumstances could it repeat the attack in any way. I also commanded that it could not attach itself to me or to any of my property and that it could never leave with me. After that, nothing else happened and the house was quiet, so I slept peacefully for the rest of the night. The next day, the house was thoroughly exorcised by someone who is a highly experienced expert in performing house clearings.

Another form of physical attack which paranormal entities can make is to leave physical scratch marks on your body. Typically, although not always, these scratch marks appear in clusters of three. This is believed to mock the Holy Trinity, although nothing has been proven about that assumption. There have been many other instances of single or double scratch marks appearing on a person's skin. This may be because the person in question doesn't have a deep-rooted religious belief.

Alternatively, they may not be a Christian in their faith. Therefore, mocking the Holy Trinity would be completely meaningless to someone of the Jewish, Hindu or Muslim faith. If the entity they're dealing with knows this, then a triple scratch wouldn't generate the same level of fear. There is absolutely no doubt that malevolent paranormal energy entities are cunning, devious, and manipulative, and they will use every trick possible to dupe you.

Foul smells are another form of physical attack which must be considered. As you'll now know from an earlier section, the sense of smell is a very reliable indicator of some form of interaction with a paranormal entity. It has been reported that foul smells can become so overpowering and chocking that they have forced investigators to leave the scene to recover their breath.

If you encounter a negative, or "evil" paranormal entity, it's almost never going to present itself as such immediately. Instead, these things almost always initially present the most benign of images. In fact, the more benign the initial appearance of the entity, then the warier I am of what it could really be, and what its real intentions are. There have been numerous recorded occasions of how someone has encountered what seems to be the spirit of a child, or a loved relative, only to later discover that it was all a masquerade to entrap you by a negative "evil" entity. It was just an act to win your trust so that it could manipulate you. It is also possible that this could be an early stage of what could be an attempted possession. Many professional investigators have also been fooled by this simple trick. It's never easy to spot, often until it's too late.

Are all paranormal entities negative and "evil" as is often claimed by those in the ghost hunting TV shows? No, of course, they're not. In fact, most of the entities I've encountered during my career as a paranormal investigator have been perfectly benign. I know that many other world-leading reputable paranormal organisations concur with me in this respect. Remember, the ghost hunting TV shows generally deliberately hype it all up to increase ratings.

If one accepts the theory of the human spirit being composed of some form of energy which continues to exist after the physical death of the human body, then there must also be other forms of energy entities that exist. if these energy entities reside in some part of the universal existence entirely in energy form, then it isn't a great leap of faith to envision how these entities can manipulate and control physical matter.

All physical matter in our world and universe is entirely composed of energy. It is a mass of atoms, electrons, protons, quarks, bosuns and probably many other particles which we have yet to identify. In theory, we humans should one day be able to manipulate physical matter too. if you can manipulate the energy and bonds which kink it all together, then it's theoretically possible to transmute objects from one form into another.

This is the sort of thing that elementals, paranormal entities, wizards and other beings have been reputed to be able to do for thousands of years. There are many paranormal energy entities which exist that are extremely dangerous and apparently possess the ability to manipulate physical objects in ways which are still baffling to us. Make no mistake, there is the potential of very real danger when dealing with paranormal energy entities.

Attachments and Possession

Paranormal energy attachments are perhaps one of the most dangerous of all attacks. There have been many recorded instances of such entities attaching themselves to someone during an investigation and following them home. A paranormal attachment is when a living person has either the energy of, the spirit of a dead person, or another unknown energy entity that has somehow become attached to them. Once attached, the entity will usually not leave until it is forced to leave. This usually takes a lot of effort and time because professional paranormal experts will need to be consulted. In the worst cases, a full exorcism may even need to be performed to get rid of the entity.

Paranormal attachments and possessions can happen at any time, and often when you'd least expect it. Wendy Walsh is a businesswoman who lives in Cheshire, England. In October 2011 she had attended a weekend business event at The Samling Hotel, on the shores of Lake Windermere in England's beautiful Lake District National Park. Wendy booked a room in the hotel for both nights of the event. The room she chose was called The Blue Room, which was one of the finest rooms in the hotel. However, at the time she booked the room, she had no idea that it was reputed to be haunted.

When I interviewed Wendy about the terrifying experience she had while staying there. During the interview, she was clearly still upset by recalling what had happened there several years ago. On the first night in the hotel, the inclement weather of the day had turned into a heavy rain beating down at the eaves of the old hotel. Soon after she had fallen asleep she was woken by what she initially believed was the storm outside. However, she became increasingly aware that the noise of the "storm" she was hearing wasn't outside the hotel at all, instead, it was somehow inside her room.

Wendy then became aware of the sound of muffled voices. At first, she thought that she was merely hearing voices from another room adjacent to her own. However, she soon realised that the voices she was hearing were in fact inside her room, and very close to where she was lying in bed. Even though she could hear two voices talking, she still couldn't clearly make out what they were saying. She described them as being as if they were “almost talking English” but it wasn’t quite the way in which we know it.

By now, Wendy was fully awake and very scared. All she could do was lay there with the bed sheets covering her face and hope that whatever it was she was hearing would eventually go away. Instead of going away, things got worse. Wendy told me that she suddenly felt a significant weight on her chest, and the pressure steadily increased to the point where it became difficult for her to breathe. By this time Wendy was literally trembling with fear wondering what would happen next.

She then felt “something” physical literally “rush” into her body at chest level. After that happened, it was as if whatever it was suddenly had taken complete control of her body. She was unable to move a muscle and couldn’t even speak, so screaming for help was completely out of the question.

To her amazement, one of the voices suddenly became legible, and she could clearly understand what it was saying. The voice said, “I can make her arms and legs move, look what happens when I do this.” It was just as if she was only hearing one half of a conversation something was having about her. At that point, she felt something controlling her leg which then made it kick out from under the bed sheets. After that, the voice said, “Look what I can make her do”, and then her right arm raised up in the air in front of her.

Whatever it was that had entered her body through her chest had taken complete control of her, and she was physically helpless. No matter how hard she tried to move or scream, her body simply wouldn't respond. All she could do was to wait and see what it would do next.

I then asked Wendy if she felt as though what she had experienced would be a similar feeling to having your car hijacked at gunpoint. To then feel like she was nothing more than a helpless passenger in the vehicle while the hijacker had total control to drive it wherever they wanted to. She told me that those were the very words she was looking for because that was exactly how it felt.

Thankfully, the next instant Wendy felt whatever it was that had been in control of her, rush out of her body in the same way that it entered. After that, the room fell silent again and the noise of the storm could only be heard outside her window once again. Once she had taken back control of her body from the entity, she didn't sleep again that night. She immediately told members of the hotel staff what had happened, and they searched her room, but unsurprisingly found nothing.

The next night, the only way she would stay in The Blue Room again was with a friend who was also attending the same business event. The night was calm, and even though Wendy could hardly sleep again, her friend slept well. Wendy is what is known as a "sensitive". This means that she is more open and susceptible than most people would be in being aware of, and monitoring paranormal phenomena. Perhaps this was why she was targeted the night before, because 'it' knew she would respond to it.

At the time of writing this book, I've only just completed the above interview with Wendy Walsh. In the coming months, I'm going to arrange to stay in the same room that she did at The Samling Hotel. When I do, it will be with a small team of experienced paranormal investigators, complete with a full array of equipment to research what paranormal entities reside there. I'll report fully about this via the "More Questions Than Answers with Adrian Lee" radio show, or MQTA for short. It can easily be found via The International Paranormal Society's (TIPS) website, via the MQTA Facebook page, on The Dark Matter Digital Network, or on Soundcloud.

Wendy was one of the lucky ones. Those who experience an attachment or a possession from a paranormal entity that leaves them of their own volition, and which doesn't have to be forced to leave. Most people aren't that lucky. There have been many recorded instances of people who have literally lost control of their bodies through possession and by paranormal attachment for long periods of time. In these cases, they even lose control of their senses, their emotions, and their mind to the negative energy attachment that has invaded them.

A negative energy attachment can cause a person to exhibit uncharacteristic behaviour including a propensity towards violence, wild mood changes, addiction, sudden rages, and other completely irrational behaviours. There have even been rare instances recorded where attachments have enabled the host to perform tasks that they were previously unable to perform such as playing an instrument, speaking another language, or skilful drawing etc.

However, these are rarities when compared to the more commonly reported negative effects. It's important to remember that an attachment could last hours, days, weeks, months, years, decades, and even a lifetime in some cases. More importantly, there is no guarantee that you will ever be able to get rid of it once it has attached itself to you. Therefore, prevention is always going to be far better than hoping to find a cure after the fact.

How can this happen? Is there any science to support the possibility of a negative attachment affecting your mind/brain? How can an energy entity take control of a human being? The answer is, much easier than one might at first think. New scientific research has finally shed light on how we humans might be vulnerable to having an energy entity take us over in part; or whole. There is now a scientific explanation about how we're "driven" as physical human bodies. More importantly, it's about how we don't actually "think" our thoughts. Instead, science has now proven that we become aware of thoughts which come from a much older and more primitive part of the brain.

The new ground-breaking research study about this was performed by Professor David Oakley of the University College London Division of Psychology and Language Sciences, and Professor Peter Halligan at the University of Cardiff. It was about human consciousness, and how our thoughts are created relating to the non-conscious systems in our brains. They found that our thoughts come from much older non-conscious systems which operate behind the scenes in our brain. Some people call this the "personal narrative" which is key to our survival instincts and isn't affected by our self-awareness.

Prior to this study, it was believed that the thoughts, beliefs, and perceptions that we all experience every day was simply part of us being a sentient human being with consciousness. In other words, our thoughts weren't our thoughts until we actually thought them. It now seems that we were very wrong in that belief.

Therefore, if we don't "think" our thoughts, then where do they come from, and what implications does this have in respect of our so-called "free-will" and being personally responsible for anything? Obviously, the results of this research study will generate a plethora of questions and sub-questions with social, moral, and possibly even legal implications. Thankfully, these matters aren't our concern, and we only must examine how these findings affect us in paranormal matters.

Since we now know that we don't actually "think" our thoughts, and instead we become aware of them, it fundamentally changes our understanding of how we're "driven" and controlled as human beings. It's now clear that we're more like either a "driver" or possibly even a "passenger" in a metaphoric car. The vehicle then becomes "aware" of our commands and ideas, including the route the vehicle is taking, rather than us deciding and "thinking" about what the route will be.

This newly discovered mechanism about how our brain operates also seems to be leading us in the right direction so that we might eventually discover how our spirit or soul operates and drives us as human beings. Since the dawn of time, religious leaders, scholars, and scientists have all struggled to better understand if, and how, we can have a human soul or spirit. More importantly, how the concept of a spirit or soul fits into the electro-biological mechanism we exist in as human animals.

Continuing with the car analogy in this respect. If a human being can be likened to a car, then the body of the car would be our human body, the engine, wheels, and control mechanisms of the car would be the organs, bones and muscles, and the electronics, steering wheel, accelerator pedal and gears would be the brain.

To expect to find the driver of the car inside the engine would be ridiculous. Therefore, it was also ridiculous for religious leaders and scientists to have expected to find our soul, or spirit inside our human brain. It just makes perfect sense that "we" as a person/spirit/soul would be positioned inside the cabin of the car. After all, the brain is merely an interface for the energy entity that is our spirit or soul. As the "driver" of our human vehicle, it now seems highly likely that the energy entity/soul/spirit that is "us", somehow generates the thoughts which we then become consciously aware of.

As an extension of this train of thought, if the energy entity that is our "spirit" is usually sitting behind the scenes inside the cabin of the car driving us, then what happens if something else gets into the metamorphic cabin of the car? Could this be the mechanism which enables people to channel a spirit? Could the human vehicle be hijacked by another energy entity? Could this be how attachments and even demonic possessions happen to people? Is this how energy entities that are dark, negative, or "evil" can either partially, or wholly take control of us as human beings? I believe that this is probably exactly how it all happens.

It could be that this ancient mechanism which we all have also somehow allows us to connect into what has been called the cosmic consciousness, or the Akashic records. In addition to this, I also believe that it is somehow connected to the frequently reported phenomenon of how people sometimes involuntarily behave illogically, such as by walking towards an alien craft during UFO encounters.

I strongly urge everyone who participates in any kind of paranormal investigation, to take very seriously the risks associated with attachment and possession. These are new frontiers which are being charted, and thankfully science is at least partially catching up to help explain and substantiate how things work. The resultant damage and fallout from any kind or paranormal attack can be both debilitating and serious. Furthermore, it can seriously adversely affect others around the person who is being attacked, especially spouses and close family members.

The Ouija Board

There are also great dangers associated with the use of the Ouija board. For some amazing reason, the Ouija board is typically sold in many western countries as a child's toy. In my opinion, this is as dangerous as selling real knives and guns to those children! The Ouija board is NOT a toy, it is a serious means of communicating with paranormal energy entities. More importantly, you usually have no idea if the entities you're communicating with are good or bad until it's too late.

Whatever you contact via the Ouija board can initially appear to be completely benign, but it's not until much later that you find out the hard way that it's positively evil. Many such instances have been well documented. Children who have run into trouble through using the Ouija board have frequently reported that whatever it was they were in contact with had initially presented itself as being another child, just like them. However, the truth of it was that it was a malevolent "dark" paranormal entity.

A good analogy of Ouija board use would be to dial a random phone number on your mobile phone. With luck, it's possible to dial the number of a random telephone box and for that ringing phone to be picked up by a passing stranger. Would you know who that person was? Of course not, because you'd only have their word to go on, and there would be no way of substantiating anything they told you.

Furthermore, once that person then knows your phone number, and they can then call you back anytime they want. However, unlike a telephone, any negative energy entity you've connected with via the Ouija board can leave the line to you wide open, with you being unable to disconnect it. More importantly, unlike a telephone, because they are an energy entity, they can then access you and your location via the link set up via the Ouija board.

Therefore, using the Ouija board can be very dangerous. 50% of the time using the Ouija board nothing bad will probably happen. However, the dangers associated with the other 50% are simply too great to risk. Therefore, I would never recommend playing with one. I also strongly urge everyone who knows a child who owns one, to warn their parents of the great danger their child/children are in.

Protecting Yourself and Total Belief

How can you protect yourself during a paranormal investigation? The answer is surprisingly simple, it's through both belief and intent. Prior to a paranormal investigation, many people who have deep-rooted religious beliefs say a prayer of protection, either as an individual or as a group.

The prayer they use will command whatever is present and/or make contact with, that it/they cannot under any circumstances attach to the people present, or to any of their equipment. Also, that it cannot leave with them under any circumstances, and that what, or whoever is there, must stay there.

Whatever you say during this prayer, and where your prayer is directed, will always entirely be dependent upon your personal spiritual beliefs. However, it's all about belief and intent. No matter who or what you pray to, it will not work if you don't completely believe that it will. Unless you believe 100%, then whatever you say or do will only be partially effective at best, or at worst, completely useless.

Many people have told me that they're not especially religious and have asked how they can still protect themselves if they aren't 100% committed to a specific religion. Once again, the answer is in 100% belief and intent. If you don't say a prayer to a deity which you completely believe in, then you must command with the same 100% belief and intent that whatever/whoever you encounter during your paranormal investigation cannot affect you, harm you or leave with you etc.

I know that many people who read this and who are deeply committed to their religion will differ with me about this. This is in the same way that those people who do not follow a religion can instead commit to their own unshakable belief and intent about something. In short, if it works for you, then that's what it's all about.

This is why when something is smudged, or cleared, using smouldering sage, it only works if total belief and intent are expressed. Otherwise, the whole process is useless. Therefore smudging/clearing can take place with things other than sage. The main reasons that sage is used in this process are because it has long been reputed to have general cleansing powers, and the aroma is nice too.

This is also where science steps in again, with research that has come to light in recent years about the power of belief and intent. There is now indisputable scientific evidence to support the power of 100% belief in something. Science has now proven that the power of total belief can even change and affect you at a cellular biological level. Your belief can either have a positive or a negative effect, the only thing that decides which this will be is you. It's all about the choice of what you wish to believe.

I'd highly recommend reading some of the excellent books by the amazing Dr Bruce Lipton. Dr Lipton is a former medical school professor and research scientist who has performed some ground-breaking studies into the power of belief. His experiments have clearly shown how our genes and DNA do not control our biology. Instead, we control it by what we think and believe. He has even shown how our very DNA is controlled by external signals. More importantly, these signals include the positive and negative signals and thoughts from our brain.

This is how powerful the power of 100% belief can be. Furthermore, this truly awesome power rests within all of us right now. Dr Lipton is now working to demonstrate his latest research in quantum physics and cellular biology which shows the that the human body can be physically changed by simply retraining our 100% committed thinking. I'm excited to learn about what he finds during his research about all this.

If belief alone can alter our cellular structure and DNA, then it can also control whatever negative energy entity attempts to hijack and possess our mind and take control of our body. I believe that 100% committed injunctions of protection both before and after any paranormal investigation are essential. They are the only certain way to protect you from anything negative and malevolent that might be lurking out there waiting for the chance to attack you.

Chapter 9: How to Perform a Paranormal Investigation

Advanced Preparation

I don't know any other way to put it, so I'll be blunt. ALL TEAM MEMBERS SHOULD BE 1st AID TRAINED RESPONDERS, AND EVERYONE SHOULD CARRY THEIR OWN BASIC 1ST AID KIT. It just makes good sense for all team members to get trained in the basics of administering first aid before they go out on any investigation.

I'd even go so far as to say that I'd expect all team members to keep themselves physically fit, especially if you do a lot of outdoor investigations, or in large buildings with lots of stairs. There's nothing more frustrating than having members of the team who are unfit to the point where they slow the investigation down to a grinding halt. They could even pose a danger to themselves if they exert themselves too much during an investigation, and potentially place the rest of the team in danger as well.

Always carry identification with you, together with official documents granting you access to investigate on the location you're at. This should be basic common sense. If you're prepared in this way, then if any member of the public spots suspicious lights in an abandoned building, then when the police arrive you can clear up any misunderstanding quickly and easily. You can verify that you have been allowed by the owners of the land/building to be there and investigate as a team.

Plan ahead, and practice how to perform basic search and rescue operations. I'm a master scuba instructor, and therefore I'm also qualified as a search and rescue dive leader and instructor. This means that I'm particularly keen to ensure that every member of a team I'm either leading, or I'm a member of, have all undergone a basic review of emergency search and rescue drills.

Team members need to know the different kinds of basic search patterns to employ, communication systems, agree on muster points and codes of practice in case of an emergency, and everyone needs to know how to use all the emergency equipment that you have brought with you. This may sound as though I'm an over-cautious person, and you'd be right because I am. I believe it's better to plan ahead to eliminate as many potential issues and threats to safety as possible. I occasionally run courses about this, and in 1st aid for paranormal investigations.

Every team member should have a reliable method of communicating with the outside world if needed. If you can't get cellular coverage either indoors or outdoors, then set up a system of time safety checks at pre-determined points and times and use walkie-talkies that work wherever you're investigating. if necessary, during an extreme outdoor investigation, at least one person should have a satellite phone for emergency use.

The next logical question which comes to mind is "Do I need insurance, and if so, what kind do I need, and what coverage should I have?" Exploring the possible need for even the most basic type of 3rd party public liability insurance is always going to be worthwhile. A team member may inadvertently break a valuable object when investigating in the dark, or even worse, they may injure themselves in some way.

More importantly, you may not even be allowed into certain places unless you have adequate insurance cover already in place. The owners of old and near derelict buildings may feel uneasy about allowing you and your team into a potentially hazardous location just in case they then make themselves liable to being sued if someone injures themselves during an investigation.

Since you can't exactly expect to find readily available online insurance cover for paranormal investigators, you'll probably have to delve into the world of loss adjustment and risk liability. This will probably mean that you must consult a specialist insurance broker. Once you have told them what you do, your qualifications, the number of people who typically comprise a team, the value of items that you use, etc. then they'll probably have to invite quotes from several large insurance companies.

Ensure that all the equipment which you and your team bring with you has been cleaned, is free from static electricity. Don't forget to only clean your camera lenses with micro fibre lens cloths. I'd recommend that you always maintain your equipment in top shape, and only use the correct cleaning procedures as designated by the manufacturer. This way you will build a solid reputation for gathering good uncontaminated evidence.

Make sure that all batteries are fully charged. If you're lucky enough to have a room which acts as a location headquarters, then set up re-charging units there as needed. It is reputed that energy entities can suddenly draw or even drain all power from batteries, therefore, it's a good idea to always bring plenty of spares with you.

Set and synchronise all equipment so that the day, date and time match. Wear the right clothes and shoes for the location and bring emergency gear with you just in case of extreme weather changes or if someone gets unexpectedly wet for some reason. Never wear clothes that generate static electricity and avoid clothes which are naturally noisy during normal use. There's nothing more annoying than listening to someone's clothes rustle every time they breathe when trying to capture uncontaminated audio or video recording. In respect of clothes in general, make sure that people don't wear shoes that are the squeaky kind, and with a sole that can cause excessive contamination of evidence simply by walking. If they do, then note it in advance so that you don't waste time pursuing a dead-end line of investigation just because someone's shoes squeak unexpectedly.

In respect of squeaks and other forms of audio contamination, it's a good idea to ensure that every team member follows the rule of tagging all contamination. For example, if someone has a rumbling tummy, then they should say aloud that it was their tummy making the noise at the point that it does. This then eliminates it as being mistaken for potential evidence. No matter what the contamination might be, always audibly tag it so that it can be eliminated when the evidence is reviewed.

Ensure that all recording and photographic devices have a clean, re-formatted hard drive/memory card that is ready to record. If you're using tape for some reason, then make sure that you have a new one in the machine, plus any spares as needed.

Torches are an essential item, especially if you're investigating at night. Even if you're investigating outdoors in daylight, it's still always wise to have several torches with you together with spare batteries. The fact is that you never know what will happen. It's always possible that someone on your team may have an accident on an outdoor location. Even if this occurs early in the day, if you're in a remote location with an extended supply line, then it could be after dark when the emergency services arrive with help. If you have no torches with you then you're in big trouble.

In addition, no matter where you're investigating, you should always take enough food and water for everyone to survive for an extended period if the need ever arose. If you don't need the supplies, which is highly likely, then there will be plenty of goodies for everyone to take home with them after the investigation has concluded. If you're investigating outdoors for an extended period of time, or on an extreme location, then it's always a good idea to double the rations of both food and water.

This then begs the next logical question, where can you relieve yourself when "nature calls" while on the investigation location? Toilet facilities must be thought about in advance, and how the noise from a rusty plumbing system might temporarily interrupt an indoor investigation in an old building.

With all the necessary training, planning, tools, and equipment in pace, then you should be ready for almost anything. More importantly, you'll be able to focus your attention on the main reason for you being there in the first place, which is paranormal investigating.

Research

It's important to rule out any possible natural or man-made occurrences that could be misinterpreted as evidence of paranormal activity. It's also important to gather as much background research as possible, prior to any physical investigation. Thorough advanced research is vital to all good investigations. The internet is obviously a good place to start, but don't just leave it at that. You should also use land registry offices to check if any names of the people listed at the property correlate with any events that were recorded in newspapers and journals of the time.

There are many documents and sources of information that aren't fully available online yet. Explore the city, town, village, church, and /or parish records. Churches are an excellent source of information, especially if you're allowed to access the archives. Newspaper offices often keep old copies of newspapers on microfilm because they haven't been converted to online documents. They also often keep print copies of old newspapers too.

In the United States and Canada, what they consider to be "old" when it comes to newspapers and church records wouldn't be considered old, and certainly not ancient by someone from Britain or Europe. At the most, the records on the North American continent go back a few hundred years to the time of and after the first settlers, so your research is limited in that. Therefore, don't forget to explore the folklore and legends of the native Americans which might contain some important additional information that might be useful.

In Britain and Europe, records and documents can be much older, and special advanced permission might be needed which might take months to be granted. The older the documented research you can perform, then the better the overall picture you will build.

I also think that it's important to explore the geological maps and surveys of the area. This can help to shed a lot of extra light on the subject, especially if there are any geological and magnetic anomalies associated with the building and the area in general. While you're doing this, it's also a good idea to check the location of any possible underground pipelines, power cables and caves as these may be sources of EMF.

For example, the Charles Manson house in California is located on an area of exceptionally high geomagnetic activity. Such activity may itself be the cause, or if not that, the amplifier needed for the paranormal activity to take place that has been recorded there.

I experienced a great deal of paranormal activity when I lived in Iceland for a short time. Iceland sits right on the mid-Atlantic trench where the tectonic plates meet. Therefore, it experiences masses of geomagnetic and Vulcanic activity as a result. I believe that this has a great deal to do with the paranormal activity that many people have experienced there over the centuries. It's an avenue of research that will require significant funding, together with open-minded scientific research to learn more about any possible correlations. Different types of rock seem to be magnifiers, enablers, or possibly even causes of some alleged paranormal activity.

Limestone is one such rock. Limestone is a sedimentary rock which is composed of the skeletal fragments of ancient marine organisms. Its major component materials are the minerals aragonite and calcite, which are crystal forms of calcium carbonate. It also seems that limestone emits a significant EMF (Electro Magnetic Field) due to the elements it contains, especially quartz. In addition, there are often many underground streams associated with limestone strata, and it is quite common to find alleged haunted locations above and around them on the earth's surface.

To conclude this section, I strongly urge you to perform thorough and detailed background research before even moving on to the next stage, which is the interview.

Interview

Now that your research is completed, together with detailing all the objectives of your proposed investigation, the next stage. This is to interview whoever owns it, and any witnesses there are to the alleged paranormal events that have taken place there. Before the interview takes place, you should pre-prepare a detailed list of questions you'd like answered before you start actively investigating. When you attend an interview it's a good idea to have a pen and notepad with you, as well as digital forms of note-taking. I find the Microsoft One Note is excellent, and whatever I write in that software automatically appears back on my laptop when I next fire it up.

Taking notes will help you to prepare for any unexpected tangents which might be worthy of exploring. If you discover a tangent like that, then guide the conversation over to it, but always make a note of where the conversation was previously heading. This way, once you've fully explored the tangent you can get back on track quickly and easily. This will also help you appear to be very organised and professional.

Remember that for many people, discussing even the possibility of paranormal activity can be very stressful and embarrassing. It's important to build a rapport with anyone you are going to interview before you begin to ask and some of the more extraordinary questions about paranormal activity. In building a rapport, it will help the interviewee to relax and open themselves up to you more easily about a subject that that may have previously faced ridicule, pain, suffering, stress, or embarrassment about.

They need to know that no matter how strange the things are that they tell you, you will believe them at face value and not judge them because of it. It's also a good idea to get to know their thoughts and beliefs about religion too. This will tell you how they would have previously perceived the notion of someone experiencing paranormal activity. The better that you get to know an interviewee, the more information you will discover about the location and the alleged activity that has been reported and/or witnessed taking place there.

Draw the interviewee into telling you all they can about the alleged events and activity in as much detail as possible. Include dates, times, what they and/or other witnesses were doing, if they know it then also include data about weather, temperature, atmosphere, etc. I always like to know exactly how the interviewee felt when they first witnessed the alleged phenomena, and how they and any other witnesses to it reacted as a result.

To help me in this, I use techniques I learned about at the BBC combined with my system of Mental Martial Arts which was published as a book in 2009. Everyone has a preferred communication bias. This is how they naturally prefer to communicate with others, and equally importantly, how they preferred others to communicate with them.

If you know what this preferred bias is, then whoever you're interviewing will automatically feel much more at ease with you, and they'll open up to you more. The signs, signals, and biases you should look for during conversations are what I call word clues. These word clues will all fall into one or more of the following categories:

- **V**isual
- **A**udible
- **T**actile or Kinaesthetic
- **O**lfactory or Gustatory
- **D**ata or Digital

Once you've identified the specific word clues and biases in your interviewee's communication, you'll begin to see a pattern forming. Soon, you'll have gained all the information needed to help you guide the direction of the conversation to gain all the information you need to know about the alleged paranormal activity. Look for words and phrases such as:

- I *see* what you mean
- I *hear* what you say
- I can *feel* it coming together
- I *smell* a rat
- I *understand* what you say

The word "clues" in each of the above phrases will tell you if your opponent falls either strongly or partially into one or more of the categories listed. Once you have identified the bias, then begin using similar words and phrases in your questions and general conversation with the interviewee. Since you'll be using the same words and phrases that they do, then this will really help to make them feel much more at ease.

There are many more techniques you can use during an interview situation, especially if you wish to perfect this at a high level. During my career, I worked with BBC TV News for over a decade, and their training was the very best there could be when it comes to effective and ethical questioning.

As a martial arts practitioner of over 45 years, I then combined these techniques with martial arts strategies and tactics to write a book called Mental Martial Arts. Details about this are in the "other books by..." section at the end of this book. It's readily available on Amazon and it has been used as required course material by some US government organisations and large companies to train their key leadership teams.

With the "commercial" over, I'll return my focus again. Either before or after the interview, if possible, walk through the location with the interviewee, and any other witnesses who are present. It would be even better if you could do this while recording the walkthrough and conversation on video.

This way they can describe events, places and things that happened complete with a visual reference. After the video walkthrough, you can make video and stills of the screen grabs to match up with your detailed notes. This will enhance the final briefings with the rest of the team.

Walkthrough

During the walkthrough phase, make sure that every member of your team has the appropriate designated equipment they need with them. Since they will have already read your research and interview notes, studied the video, photographs and map, you're then all prepared to compile the final sitemap.

Double check that everyone on your team has turned their cell phones onto flight mode, turned off unnecessary electronic devices such as fitness trackers, cellular-connected watches, or other electronic watches that emit a radio signal and could interfere with sensitive detection equipment.

This new map is the one that you'll use as your final location investigation guide. You need to include data about specific areas of interest, proposed equipment locations, the direction equipment sensors and lenses should face. The map should also include information about any live power points, fuse boxes, gas and water pipes, smoke alarms, as well as anything which might be hazardous or cause potential contamination.

Make notes about everything, the more detail the better. Begin at the doorway and work your way from there through the building. As you perform the walkthrough, measure and record your baseline readings. These should include all the basics, such as temperature and EMF activity etc. It's also a good idea to make a video recording of any locations of interest during the walkthrough.

Check for and record any light anomalies from vehicles or beacons, together with vibrations from the road or any other external source. Certain types of wall surface, placards, glass, and/or signs can cause reflections and issues when using flash photography. If the location isn't in a good state of repair, then this can cause issues. This includes the overall expansion and contraction of the building and wooden boards, draft from old windows, rusty door hinges, plumbing pressure and pipe issues, and insect and vermin infestation. All of these things can seriously contaminate and compromise any evidence you gather.

If there is a central heating system still in use, or if there are any other domestic or industrial devices that are still operative and can make noise, note them down. Preferably render these things inoperative, at least while you perform the investigation. Air vents are always going to pose a potential problem, especially if they can't be effectively close-off and sealed.

Take particular notice of any potentially drafty doors and windows, together with their frames. Note down what type of construction and design they are. Are there any curtains still hanging? Are there any old window blinds that can cause possible noise contamination in some way?

The type and condition of the floor in a building will create a wide range of potential problems. Certain types of carpet can cause static issues, laminate flooring can be squeaky, and concrete floors littered with debris can cause crunches and other noise. Wooden floorboards in rooms overhead, especially in attics can allow dust to fall when people walk on them, which is a problem if video or stills photography is taking place in the room below. This can look like the presence of orbs and it makes the process of sifting through evidence even more challenging and time-consuming after the investigation is over.

If you're investigating an exterior location, then this raises many other interesting issues which must be dealt with and noted. To begin with, when you draw maps and plans of the area you should always include accurate compass directions. If there are buildings in the investigation area, then note down all the materials they are made of. Remember that corrugated steel roofing can cause noise due to expansion and contraction, as can wood. Wooden shutters and old wooden steps can be problematic too, as can exterior metal water or central heating oil tanks.

What is the ground surface composed of? Is there any shale of gravel areas that can cause noise contamination? What about wind noise and foliage in the area? Will the trees creak? Will bushes rustle? Will unstable buildings shift and creak due to the current weather conditions?

There may be contamination from animals too. Some of these may have dug deep and complex tunnels which stretch for a considerable distance. Depending on which country you're investigating it, then each will have its own unique issues in this respect. For example, in Britain, animal contamination may be caused by foxes, squirrels or badgers, whereas in the United States animals like a racoon, gophers, snakes, and coyotes must be considered.

Are there any streams or drains running through the area? If so, how close are they and how might they cause potential noise contamination? What about electrical power lines overhead, cables below ground, and the large transformer boxes which step-down the mains power from the national grid? Some large industrial locations have several of these things, and even though the electricity supply to the buildings might be turned off, it doesn't mean that the transformer boxes aren't still live.

It is important to note everything down to help eliminate as many potential sources of contamination to your data/evidence as possible. Here is an excellent example of how thorough you must be in eliminating and explaining all possible sources of external contamination before drawing a paranormal conclusion to a phenomenon.

Staff at Manchester Museum in England once thought that an ancient Egyptian relic they had on display to be haunted. The panic was caused by a 10-inch tall 4,000-year-old relic which is an offering to the Egyptian God Osiris who was the "God of the Dead".

The statue would physically turn itself around 180 degrees to face the rear of the cabinet over a period of several days. The staff at the Manchester University Museum even filmed it turning 180 degrees on a time-lapse recording. This was despite it being locked in a sealed glass display case. The museum curator, Mr Campbell Price, was quoted in the media as saying, "I noticed one day that it had turned around, I thought it was strange because it is in a case and I am the only one who has a key. I put it back, but then the next day it had moved again." It seemed even more strange because the

"Moving" Statue of Egyptian God Osiris in Manchester Museum

statue would turn a maximum of 180 degrees so that it directly faced the prayer parchment which was displayed at the rear of the cabinet.

It was even rumoured in the media that it might be some sort of "curse" of the pharaohs. As you can imagine, the media ran wild with stories about the "haunted artefact", together with suspected other kinds of paranormal attachments to the artefact. At this point, the world-famous physicist professor Brian Cox O.B.E. was among the many experts who were consulted about the mysterious happenings. He is a professor of particle physics in the School of Physics and Astronomy at the University of Manchester. Eventually, through a scientific process of elimination, researchers found that there was a perfectly logical explanation for the mystery. Professor Cox thought that it was something known as differential friction. This was because the base of the artefact was

"Moving" Statue of Egyptian God Osiris in Manchester Museum, June 2018

very slightly curved. However, this was almost invisible to the naked eye and was only discovered when examined in the laboratory.

They then checked for external vibration sources and found that heavy double-decker buses passing every few minutes outside the building produced enough low-level vibration to interact with the slightly curved base of the artefact. The result was that this was the reason why the relic appeared to "paranormally" turn itself around. It had a perfectly logical explanation. This is an excellent example of why you should always thoroughly check for and eliminate all possible external contamination sources together with microscopic anomalies to objects.

With all the initial pre-investigation steps successfully completed, you should now be ready for the next phase, the investigation. Unfortunately, this isn't simply a case of just charging into the location while taking pictures like a foreign tourist visiting a national attraction while at the same time hoping that a ghost will show up and say "Hello". This would be like deciding to hold an impromptu party in the deli section of your local supermarket and thinking that it's OK. If there are intelligent energy entities that are drawn to "reside" in that location, then they could see action like that as an unwelcome invasion.

The Investigation

With all the interview, the planning, the research and all other preliminary work completed, you're now at the stage when the real investigation can take place.

You now need to decide if you're going to stick together and investigate as a group, or if you'll split up into teams. Naturally, this will depend upon how many of you there are in a group, the size of the location you're investigating, and the amount of equipment you have. The question of breaking into different teams will also depend on if it will potentially cause the cross-contamination of data by having more than one team investigate in a small location. Once the team question has been decided, double check all walkie talkies/coms for function properly, and their remaining battery life. Then, set up all fixed position equipment at the pre-determined points you've chosen.

Use a detailed deployment list. This makes the retrieval and packing of the equipment much easier after the investigation is over. It also helps to prevent you from forgetting something by mistake. Make sure that all equipment is functioning correctly, and if it needs it, then have plenty of battery power available or uninterrupted mains power connected.

When you begin the investigation, you should once again take more baseline readings. These can then be double checked against the initial readings that were taken when you performed the walkthrough with the client/location owner and checked against those taken during the pre-investigation walkthrough with your team.

If possible, try to duplicate an event that was described to you by the people who have witnessed paranormal activity there. In addition, if an event happened during your investigation, then follow the science and if possible attempt to recreate it again.

I believe in following your instincts when taking photographs. If something makes you “feel” the urge to take a picture in a certain direction, then take it and go with the flow. Digital cameras have the enormous advantage of being able to take hundreds or even thousands of pictures if the memory card is big enough. However, the disadvantage to this is that the more pictures you take, then the more there are that will need to be examined for evidence after the investigation is over. People frequently forget that most of the work takes place after the investigation has ended, during the time-consuming process of reviewing the evidence. When using a camera, it’s best to always take two pictures with flash in close succession to each other and in the same direction. This comparison method will greatly increase your chances of capturing any anomalies.

When it comes to photographs, especially in reviewing evidence, people sometimes see faces where faces don’t exist. I’m sure that everyone has heard about this phenomenon in some form or another. For example, for centuries, people have seen the face of Jesus or The Virgin Mary in things as mundane as tea leaves, bread, baked beans, and clouds, etc. Not to mention the countless numbers of people who claim to have seen a vision of Elvis lurking in the bubbles of their bathtub or kitchen sink.

Other examples of this phenomenon are perceiving that the craters and rocks on the Moon make a face, or when the face and figure of a commonly imagined image of Jesus apparently forms in the clouds. Since the same phenomenon can also include hearing hidden messages within recorded music played normally, in reverse or at a different speed, it has serious implications for those interpreting Electronic Voice Phenomena (EVP) incorrectly.

This phenomenon is technically called pareidolia, and although it's common, scientists knew very little about it and why it happens until quite recently. Pareidolia typically occurs because the part of the brain that is responsible for seeing faces can mistakenly interpret an object, shape, or configuration with perceived "face-like" features as being an actual face. The phenomenon is connected to something called Apophenia, which is the tendency to perceive connections and meaning between completely unrelated things.

Research into this suggests that it's actually very common for people to see non-existent faces in mundane things. This is because the human brain is specifically wired to recognise faces. This means that even if there is only a suggestion of facial features being present in a picture, then the brain automatically interprets it as a face.

This all poses a serious problem for paranormal investigators. When reviewing photographic or video evidence, it means that good paranormal investigators must be extra-objective and maintain that level of objectivity when reviewing all evidence. Being interested in paranormal investigation and phenomena means that to some degree, you "want" to believe. Therefore, we must all always temper our desire in this respect with hard scientific objectivity.

Before an EVP (Electronic Voice Phenomena) recording session, make sure that you establish a reasonable period of silence before asking any questions. Don't forget to tag anything and anyone both audibly and visually if possible if something or someone accidentally contaminates the data that you're gathering.

The object of an EVP session is to capture voices on digital recordings that are inaudible to the human ear alone. Therefore, by asking a constant wall of questions without leaving a respectable break between them will yield nothing except complete confusion and contaminated evidence. What if there is an energy entity trying to communicate with you, and yet doesn't have a great deal of energy to do so. It might take a short time after a question has been asked before enough energy can be generated to give a response. If you are still talking when the response comes, then you're wasting everyone's time. Besides, it's just basic bad manners to fire a continuous stream of questions. You'd never do this to another human being, so why would you do it to a spirit, ghost, or anything else?

It's important to remember that the more EVP recorders you have deployed, then the greater the length of time it will take to review what they have recorded after the investigation has ended. If an investigation involves 3 EVP sessions, and if each last for an hour, and there are 2 recorders present at each session, then this is 6 hours of material to review. That's a huge time commitment when it comes to reviewing the audio evidence alone.

Therefore, it's always a good idea for each member of the team to take responsibility for reviewing either a certain type or a certain amount of evidence. This will spread the work, speed up the review process, and help to ensure that important evidence isn't missed. If the responsibility all falls to one person, they will soon tire under such a massive workload. Once that happens it's very easy to inadvertently overlook something important.

It's not worth using a ghost box on an investigation if you don't take good notes, and the sessions aren't recorded. There's no point in potentially witnessing excellent evidence using these devices, and then after the investigation, you have no recording to help validate what happened. Therefore, make sure that both EVP and ghost box sessions will always be properly logged and recorded.

If you gain responses to your questions, or just receive communication in general on a ghost box, then it's important to maintain total objectivity. This is also true when reviewing EVP recordings. Just as with the phenomenon of Pareidolia when it comes to reviewing photographs, it's very easy to hear voices and words that aren't really there in the audio recordings. If there are several people present during a ghost box session, then it's better for each of them to make independent notes silently about what they hear, and then compare them afterwards.

Similarly, when reviewing EVP recordings, these should be performed in a similar way. They should merely be noted by the reviewer as "Anomaly 01", "Anomaly 02" etc., and not be named according to what they "think" was said. Later, when reviewing the EVP's as a group after the investigation is over, each member of the team should once again make silent independent notes, and refrain from saying aloud what they "think" they hear. If they don't, then group auto-suggestion might take place, and the team might all be led to believe that specific words came through which don't really exist. This will always be a much more objective and scientific approach.

Make sure that every team member makes good notes throughout the investigation. Don't over complicate them, always keep them simple but to the point. Record lots of objective useful data rather than lots of waffling about "feelings". Include an objective description of any activity you encounter, the location, the time of occurrence, witnesses who were present, temperature, EMF, geomagnetic, compass, and Mel Meter readings etc.

It's a good idea to have all members of the team regularly re-check and record new baseline data on a comparison chart you can prepare in a spreadsheet and print in advance. This way it is easy to spot any significant changes and correlate them with any other data that might be recorded simultaneously. It may even be possible to prepare a graph of measurements and how they fluctuate over the course of the investigation.

Once the investigation is underway, it's very easy to simply forget about double checking the battery status of the fixed deployment electronic equipment. Therefore, it's a good idea to schedule battery checks at regular intervals and have at least two people work together on this.

If you have divided your team up into different groups, then it's a good idea to rotate them at regular intervals. This keeps everyone fresh and alert and prevents objective staleness setting in. it's worth remembering that energy entities may respond more actively to certain people, so rotating the groups will help in this respect too.

Communication

If you're able to establish communication with an energy entity via a ghost box, an Ovilus or other such devices, then what should you say? This is an excellent question. Over the years Helen and I have been on countless investigations. Almost always when on 3rd party investigations we've been frequently frustrated by people repeatedly making one of the most basic mistakes in paranormal investigation.

When asking a question while attempting to open communication, the questions almost always go something like this. "Is there anybody there?", "Who are you?" "When did you die?", "How old are you?", "What year did you die?" "Is there anyone else there with you?" On face value, there's seemingly nothing assumptive or out of the ordinary in any of those questions. Or is there?

Why should you simply assume that who or whatever it is that you're communicating with is the spirit of a person? The fact is that you've no idea if you're communicating with something that was once human, or not. Even though it's highly likely that you will be communicating with the spirit or energy of someone who has died, there is no certainty in that. Our planet is nothing more than a large ball of rock flying through space as we rotate around our sun, and our solar system is also rotating as part of our galactic cluster.

Since our planet first became habitable, who knows what beings have visited us from other worlds, or what entities have made their home here unseen to mankind since our planet was born. Mankind hasn't even been on this planet very long in geological terms. Therefore, to me at least, it seems absurd that some people arrogantly believe that humans are the only intelligent creatures that exist and there are no other intelligent lifeforms in the entire universe except us. People who think like that have lost all perspective on what we really are, and where we inhabit. Perhaps they never had any real perspective in the first place... If you're religious, then by default you're acknowledging the existence of other entities that exist in addition to human beings.

When it comes to objective paranormal investigating, I always believe that one should always begin by introducing yourself, your name, where you are from, and why you are there. I certainly wouldn't answer some strange person if I didn't at least get an introduction. Begin asking questions in a friendly but firm voice such as, "What are you?" "What kind of being are you?" "Do you have a name and if so what is it?" "Where do you come from?" "Do you come from this planet we call earth?" "if not, which planet do you come from?" "Where is this located, and in what star cluster?" "Are you from this dimension?" "if not, then what is your dimension of origin, does it have a name and how do you access it?" "Please identify what species you are, and your place/planet of origin."

Depending on the answers you get, and if you have apparently contacted the spirit of a deceased person, then you could then go into some details such as, "How old are you?", "When did you die?", "How old are you now?", "What year did you die?", "Is there anyone else there with you?" etc.

In my humble opinion, it's well worth asking some of these questions. It makes no sense to me whatsoever to always assume that whatever we communicate with was once human. As paranormal investigators, then by default, we're supposed to have an open mind. We should be open to the possibility of life in other dimensions, on other planets, non-human life and intelligence, pure energy entities, and entities of both good and evil. I'm sure that there are a great many other possibilities that I've not listed there, and yet should be included. Since there are so many possibilities of what you might be communicating with, and where they might be from, DON'T MAKE ASSUMPTIONS!

We already know that there are duplicitous and malevolent energy entities out there which only want to deceive you, so don't help them in this. Set the example in always using good, objective questioning, and pick up and directly challenge any incongruities that crop up. Make your questions friendly and respectful, yet at the same time be firm and in command of the situation. Don't allow yourself to be scared or bullied in any way. Remember the golden rule about always maintaining 100% belief in your control over any interaction, and in your absolute safety.

Be respectful during all means of communication, no matter what you're ultimately communicating with. Politely invite them to physically appear, and to be in your photographs too. If you wish, you can also invite them to use some of your spare batteries to draw energy from if they need to. However, never invite them into you, or to use you or anyone else in your team in any way whatsoever. If they respond to your requests, then always thank them for that. When you eventually conclude the session and when you leave, then politely thank them once again for communicating with you.

If there is an apparition of any sort, objects move in front of you, or anything else which could constitute an interaction with a paranormal entity, then it is important to record and note as much basic data about it as possible.

It's common that when several people witness the same car accident, each of them will have a different account of what happened after the event. The same is true of events that happen during a paranormal investigation. Even though several team members may be only a few feet apart when they witness the same thing and/or event, it's highly likely that each of them will have a slightly different account of it when the notes are finally compared afterwards.

Therefore, each team member should write their own notes silently and independently, without cross consultation with other team members about what happened. When you make notes and collate everyone's individual accounts, make sure that you tag them with their names. Always stick to the facts and data when writing about anything.

Once the investigation has been concluded, then de-rig all the equipment you have used. Follow your equipment checklist in reverse order. This way, whatever was deployed will be packed away and accounted for.

Never attempt to voluntarily perform any sort of clearing or any type of exorcism of the location. This is a very different matter to simply performing a paranormal investigation, and it's not something that should be attempted by an amateur. Besides, if there is something benign present, then what right have you to remove it of your own volition? None... If there is a seriously disturbing paranormal or poltergeist activity taking place there, and if the owner desires it to be cleared, then make sure that only the most experienced professionals do this.

If you don't have the required skills or experience to do it properly, then you could easily end up increasing the level of activity that is taking place instead of eliminating it. Don't allow your ego to get the better of your good judgment. When it comes to performing proper clearings and exorcism, it is something that you must apprentice in. Only when you have gained sufficient experience under professional guidance will your teacher tell you if, or when, you're ready to go it alone.

Never attempt to draw any conclusions whilst on location, even if the owner is there with you and is anxious to know what you've discovered. just politely tell them that you need to properly process and evaluate all the evidence that has been gathered. Once that is done, then you'll set up a dedicated time and place to meet with them to go through it all. It's not very professional to commit yourself to say that something paranormal is taking place unless you have eliminated every other logical possibility.

Never forget what Sir Arthur Conan Doyle wrote the great detective Sherlock Holmes as saying in chapter 6 of the book, "The Sign of Four" in 1890. *"When you have eliminated the impossible, whatever remains, however improbable, must be the truth."*

With all team members accounted for, and all the equipment safely packed away, then gather the team closer together. This is the point at which you then recant another statement or prayer of protection. Say it aloud in a firm voice as you make it very clear that nothing can attach to anyone present, or to any of your equipment, and that there is no question of anything leaving there with you in any way whatsoever. Finally, always leave the location exactly as you found it.

Evaluation and Presentation of Data

With the data gathering phase over, next comes the backbone work of paranormal investigation, the evaluation of data in preparation for presentation and publishing. Unfortunately, the increasing number of TV shows in recent years covering anything with a paranormal twist only shows the "fun" side, which is being out on location investigating strange locations while ghost hunting. Many newcomers to the world of paranormal investigation have been enticed into it through watching TV shows. It often comes as a shock when they learn that they also need to commit an even greater portion of their time to evaluate the data that was gathered in the field.

Frequently, the quantity of data means that even if the data analysis workload is shared with other team members it still takes a considerable time to analyse it fully. Don't cut corners at this stage. If you do, then you're wasting the time everyone has committed to the preparation work and the investigation itself. More importantly, you'll eventually build up a reputation for being unprofessional, unscientific, and unworthy of consulting as paranormal investigators.

The first stage of any post-investigation data evaluation process would be to transfer all the digital files to a computer. When you do so, please ensure that you make notes about what equipment it was captured on, the settings that were used, together with the location, date and time for each file.

Video and stills photos always contain this information embedded within their encoded data. The way to access this information is by looking at the "properties" folder of the file. On a PC this is found by first clicking once with the left mouse button on the icon for the file, and then clicking once with the right mouse button. This will then open a message on your screen. Simply look at each tab, and make sure that you scroll down to the bottom of each tab to make sure that you don't overlook any important data in the lower sections.

It's worth investing in some good video and audio editing software to use during the review procedure. Audacity is a free audio editing software program that works very well. It will clearly show the waveform of every sound that has been captured. An audio waveform is an image on the screen that represents the audio signal of a recording.

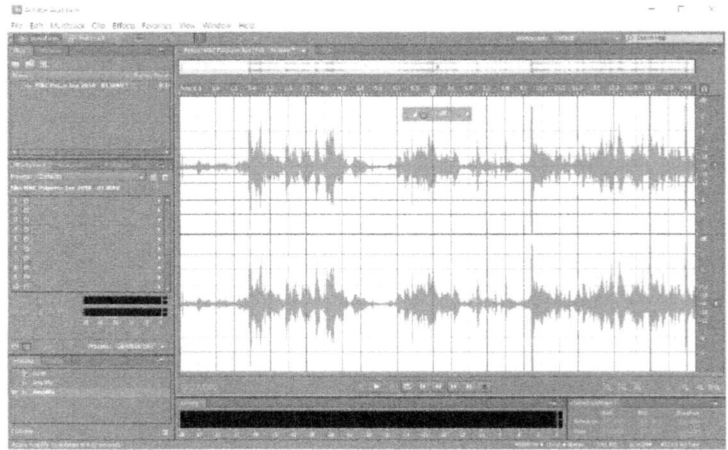

An audio file waveform in Adobe Audition

The peaks, troughs, spikes and dips etc. that can be seen on the screen shows the changes in volume/amplitude over a certain amount of time. If there are none of these, and only a perfectly flat line is displayed, then there is nothing that has perceivable been recorded. However, this doesn't necessarily mean that there might not be something recorded that is incredibly faint. Therefore, don't be tempted to skip over these sections.

You can zoom in and out on screen as needed to examine various time periods either more closely or as a wider overview. When you spot something unusual you can then zoom in on just that section to examine it in more detail. If necessary, you can then increase or decrease the volume of just that section as needed. You can also clean up some of the anomalous background noise if needed as well. You can then save the file with any changes as a new file so that the original is preserved. Then you can save the interesting sections which you feel constitute "evidence" as stand-alone audio files.

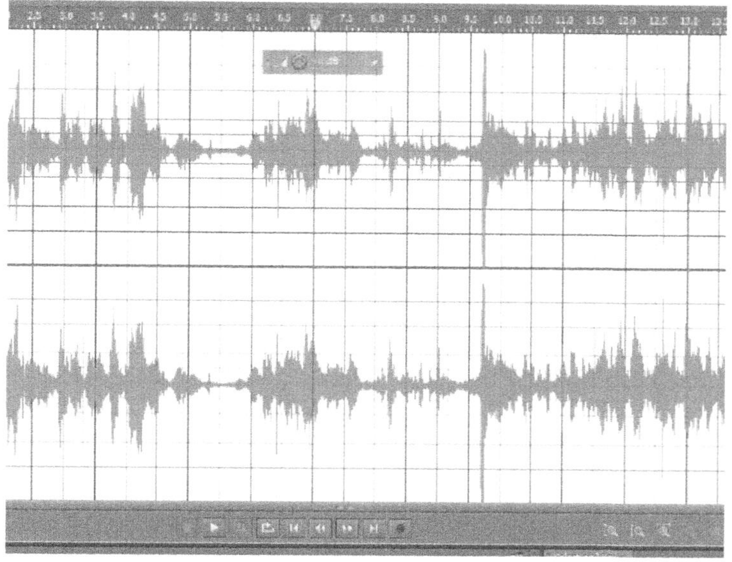

An audio file waveform close-up in Adobe Audition

If you want to save recordings as an MP3 when using Audacity, then you will need to download and install an additional 3rd party extension which allows you to do this. Other excellent software I'd highly recommend is Adobe Audition and Sony's Sound Forge. My personal preference is Adobe Audition, and the people we work closely with always use the entire Adobe Creative suite toolbox. I also use this because even though I paid a lot of money for Sony's Sound Forge, when they changed versions, they wouldn't allow me to continue using their old version again. This was despite the fact that I had the correct access/activation code which they had sent when I originally bought it. Therefore, Adobe now gets my vote.

The Adobe Creative Suite package includes the excellent video editing software, Premiere, and the trusty Adobe Photoshop programs. Since all Adobe files integrate nicely with each other, it makes it easy to seamlessly swap files between different programs. It's also possible, and almost as easy, to perform audio waveform analysis in their video editing software. It clearly shows the audio waveform and any section can be easily exported as a stand-alone file. Using the Adobe system, you can save any file in all the most commonly supported computer file formats, so you currently don't need to download or link to any add-ons.

If your budget is limited, then you can download AVS Video Editor. This is a good free program that you can use to analyse your data. However, as with all "free" programs, be careful when downloading them. This is because some download sites make you install masses of annoying spam advertising files that can fill up and even overtake your system to make it virtually unusable. Remember that "free", is never really free, and there is always a price of some sort to pay. If a program is "free", then you'll probably be subjected to lots of tacky advertising bombarding you when you least expect it, or worse. If you want to be reminded of the real price of "free" software, then just look at how the "free" Gmail service harvests and owns absolutely EVERYTHING you write and send via their system. Always fully read the "terms and conditions" of all "free" programs before using them, and/or thoroughly research the pros and cons online.

Your standard computer software will allow you to zoom in and closely examine all the stills photos you have. Some comprehensive operating systems such as Windows 10 virtually eliminate the need for a 3rd party photo editing package. In that package, you can draw on the screen to make notes in different colours, zoom, crop and save sections with unusual features that you believe to be valid data to save and present.

Physically printing the photo files on paper is one of the best ways to properly evaluate each picture in detail. You can then use a magnifying glass to examine the fine detail. One highly experienced member of the Minnesota Paranormal Research Society (MPRS) team, Marilyn Halverson has become known more commonly as "Marilyn the Magnifier" due to her excellent and extensive work in detailed photo analysis using a magnifying glass. Using physical prints together with her magnifying glass, Marilyn has been able to discover many unexplained and fascinating anomalies from dozens of investigations. Without using this technique then it's highly likely that some excellent evidence would have been completely missed. Thank you very much for all of your excellent work Marilyn!

As a rule of thumb, I always recommend that two people should work together to analyse every part of the data. This way, more detail might be spotted that might have been missed if only one person was working alone. Always remember that when you get tired, and your eyes get tired and sore, it is very easy to make simple mistakes. Working as a two-person team always has a huge bonus factor, because it will be a lot more fun to work this way. If one of you finds something unusual, I'd advise that both of you then independently research an evaluate it before you share notes and ideas about it. Only then should you begin to draw conclusions which can be added into the final presentation or publication of results.

Once you have the analysis of each silo of information complete, then begin the cross-checking process. For example, if you find an EVP captured on an audio recorder file, then find the same time-spot on the corresponding video file to see if it is there as well. Similarly, if you find an EVP on your video timeline, then cross-check that with any audio-only files that have been captured in the same vicinity. If you find corresponding data in both mediums, then this will be a real bonus which will add strength to the validation of your evidence.

It's a little more time-consuming and challenging, but if you find an anomaly in any of your video files, then also double check any stills photos that may have been taken at the same time in that location. Noting the embedded time and date data is be important during the evidence review process in general, but especially when crosschecking different files like this.

Once you and the team have collated and fully analysed all the data which was gathered during the investigation, then you can arrange an agreeable time and place to communicate your results to others. You should always be prepared to present everything in a thorough and detailed way. However, you should also be sensitive to the person/people you are presenting to. Some of them may only require an overview, while others might enjoy more detail. The best way is to be prepared and be receptive to adapt as needed. This way, if you conclude something, then you have data evidence to substantiate your conclusion should it ever be required.

A good way to make your presentation of evidence is by using a PowerPoint presentation with audio and video included at appropriate points. You can also have printed notes too. In addition to the main presentation, it's always good to have an additional one prepared which describes the scientific processes in detail that you used during the investigation. This will significantly help to raise your perceived level of professionalism and credibility in a more academic environment. As part of this, I'd also advise that you show how thorough you've been in your attempts to rationally explain things that were captured. This shows that you simply didn't "jump to conclusions" about any sort of paranormal activity taking place.

Finally, prepare a nicely bound printed document to leave with the owner of the location that you investigated. Also, let them know that if they have any further questions then they can contact you at any time in the future. Make sure that they understand that, no question is silly if you honestly don't know the answer to it.

Chapter 10: Conclusion

Paranormal phenomena in general, and especially ghosts, apparitions and hauntings, have fascinated billions of people over the centuries. The fact is that almost everyone if they're brave enough to admit it, would love to have it proven beyond doubt that ghosts categorically exist. This shouldn't be very surprising, especially since countless religions have constantly tried to convince, placate, and reassure people with the concept of an afterlife.

I believe that it is only a matter of time until enough hard, irrefutable evidence is gathered that will prove their existence. Furthermore, it will be evidence that will stand up to the most rigorous scientific examination.

Traditional science has made some remarkable progress in recent times. There have been many new discoveries made that directly impacts and helps to substantiate the beliefs and claims that paranormal investigators have been supporting for decades. Maybe the scientists who have made these remarkable discoveries haven't "joined all the dots" yet to fully understand the enormous ramifications their work is having in paranormal circles. I believe that one day soon traditional scientists will at least begin to ask questions which were once only asked by paranormal investigators.

It's also worth remembering that during their lifetime, many traditional scientists will encounter events which will make them second guess their automatic dismissal of ghosts and other paranormal entities existing. It also seems completely irrational that many traditional scientists will purport to hold deep religious beliefs, and yet dismiss the possibility of ghosts being a real phenomenon. If they had actually read the Bible, the Torah, the Upanishads, the Guru Granth Sahib or whatever other books were sacred to their preferred religion, then they could hardly miss what these books contain. They contain countless encounters with ghosts, spirits, beings from the sky, flying chariots, transmutations, beings from other worlds who can fly, flying machines of all kinds, teleportation, strange energy sources, benevolent alien beings, positive energy entities, and negative evil entities.

It's simply impossible to miss all of the aforementioned phenomena in the Bible and the sacred books and texts of other religions. Furthermore, some of these books and texts contain extremely detailed accounts of these things. In many ways, it could be argued that they are some of the best ancient reference books on UFO's, ghosts, energy entities, and paranormal activity in general.

I believe that we all go on in spirit form, even after our physical death on this planet. If you're basically a good person, then your energy signature will be positive and attracted to the positive collective. However, if you're bad, then your energy signature will end up with the greater negative energy collective.

An excellent account of how good or bad human spirits are attracted after death to either a positive or negative energy collective was by a scientist of all people. It was given by Dr Eben Alexander III who is a Harvard University neurosurgeon. Prior to his own experience, he dismissed the possibility of near-death experiences (NDE's) as being both physiologically and psychologically explainable. However, in 2008, Dr Alexander contracted a deadly form of fungal meningitis which sent him into a deep coma. During the week that he technically "died", it seems that even though his brain wasn't working at all as we know it, it was still somehow functioning at a deeper level which we don't yet understand. His experience reported that he went on to live again in a form other than human. He was conscious of an immense void, with one part being the darkest black, and the other part "brimming with light." He also reported that he was conscious that initially, he was an energy form, a nebulous jelly-like substance that was being drawn into the collective of light, the positive energy collective. More importantly, he was also conscious of other beings, of other energy forms like his own, except those were being drawn into the darkness of the void and to the negative energy collective.

It's well worth reading the book he wrote about his experiences, it makes fascinating reading. When you extract the religious trimmings from it, I believe that this is perhaps one of the most accurate descriptions about what happens after we physically die that there has ever been recorded. Dr Alexander also applies a good deal of scientific perspective to his experience, which only serves to add weight to what he describes during the time he was technically brain-dead.

As I mentioned in earlier chapters, I believe that our universe and dimension are only a fraction away from the next dimension, and it is this dimension that which we step into when we physically die. The spirit that sits in the "passenger cabin" of the vehicle which controls us, the human animal, via the oldest parts of our brain is naturally directly connected to these other dimensions.

For these reasons alone, as well as for many others too numerous to include in this concluding section of the book, I believe that modern paranormal investigators have an increasingly important role to play. The many paranormal investigators all over the world who approach the subject seriously and scientifically will one day soon help to make the breakthroughs we need. These will be the links and validations to the many new discoveries that are being made by traditional scientists that support the existence of paranormal phenomena and psychic ability. The more experience we all gain as paranormal investigators, together with the solid scientific data gathered through good experimentation, then the closer we'll eventually get to find answers to mysteries that mankind has wondered about since the dawn of time.

I would like to applaud all of the people out there who are brave enough to describe themselves as being paranormal investigators, no matter what ridicule and criticism they face from other people. You are the people who will eventually help to make the difference. You will painstakingly help to gather the important evidence needed to finally conceive the world about the many paranormal phenomena that we all believe exists.

To quote my good friend, the great paranormal researcher, broadcaster, psychic and author, Adrian Lee, "There are more questions than answers."

www.MajorVision.com

Other books by Brian Sterling-Vete and Helen Renée Wuorio

The Haunting of Lilford Hall™ - The Birthplace of the United States as a Nation Haunted by the Man Behind The Pilgrim Fathers.

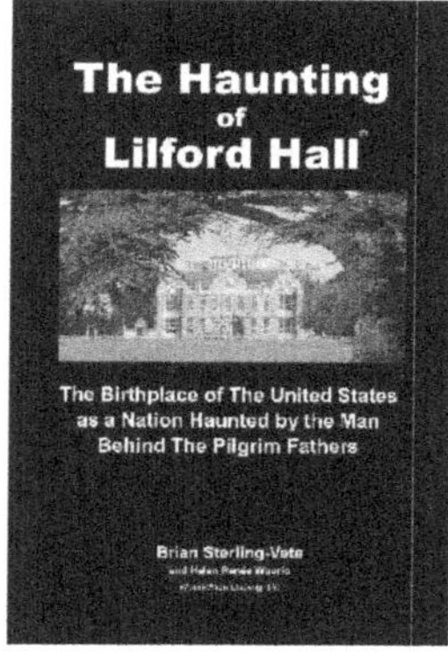

The Haunting of Lilford Hall is one of the most baffling cases ever recorded of paranormal activity experienced simultaneously by multiple people. Between 2012 and 2013, a team of 13 people came together to produce a historical TV documentary, not a paranormal investigation. The TV documentary was about the life of Robert Browne, the man who was behind The Pilgrim Fathers sailing on The Mayflower to settle the first civilian colony on the American continent. In fact, without Robert Browne, there may never have been the United States of America, at least not as we know it today.

- Robert Browne was the man who separated church from state in the reign of Queen Elizabeth 1st which is the underpinning of the United States.
- Robert Browne's words are written into the constitution of the United States.
- Robert Browne's direct descendent officially fired the first shot in the American war of independence.
- Robert Browne's beloved Lilford Hall estate was the home of President George Washington's Mother.
- Robert Browne's beloved Lilford Hall estate was the home of President Quincy Adams' family.

Just like in a typical horror movie plot, the TV crew of 13 unsuspecting people were thrust into the middle of baffling and extensive paranormal activity. They experienced doors that refused to stay closed, they had debris thrown at them, they had a door silently ripped away from the hinges and doorframe while they were in the next room. There were even several recorded multi-witness apparitions of a man fitting Robert Browne's recorded description. It is believed by many that the ghost of Robert Browne, the "Grandfather" of the United States as a nation, still haunts Lilford Hall to this day.

The 70 Second Difference™ - The Politically Incorrect, Occasionally Amusing, and Brutally Effective Guide to Strength, Fitness and Better Health.

This book has been approved by **TWiEA** – The World Isometric Exercise Association (www.TWiEA.com).

This book is a science-based no-nonsense guide that tells it straight about the most efficient ways to exercise, build muscle and get strong. Many people who aren't open-minded enough to be comfortable with new ideas and change may even consider this book to be controversial. It pulls no punches about how your deliberate lifestyle choices directly affect your body weight, overall health, fitness, strength and body shape. Lack of time is typically the enemy of regular exercise routines. However, through science-based exercise sessions lasting as little as just 70 seconds a day and needed little or no equipment, you get into shape and build your strength. It is written in a refreshing, mildly amusing and often politically incorrect style for those who aren't perpetually offended by straight talk and who want to get real results without wasting their time. It also reveals what many commercial organisations don't what you to know about how much protein you really need and the real danger of dairy products, and meat. Recommended Equipment: 2 x Iso-Bows® available on Amazon or direct from Bullworker.com

The ISOmetric Bible™ - Exercise Anywhere with Scientifically Proven Isometrics.

This book has been approved by **TWiEA** – The World Isometric Exercise Association (www.TWiEA.com).

At 335 pages, the ISOmetric Bible™ is one of the most complete, scientific, practical, and user-friendly books on isometrics that's ever been written. Isometrics have been proven by science to grow muscle and strength faster and more efficiently than any other exercise system. However, isometrics are also one of the most misunderstood forms of exercise, even by fitness professionals, coaches and personal trainers. With isometrics you can exercise your entire body in only minutes each day, they set you free to exercise anywhere and everywhere you choose, on a plane, in a car, or even while you're at work. You don't need any special equipment to get a great total-body workout, but the book shows you how to use easy to find everyday objects such as walking poles, broom handles, rope and towels to exercise with. Exercise performance science expert Brian Sterling-Vete is a veteran exercise and strength coach who was ranked among the top 10 fitness coaches in the United States in 2105. He is also considered by many to be one of the world's leading authorities on isometric exercise. Brian has trained multiple national and world champions including 2 x World Martial Arts Champion Stuart Hurst, and 4 x Time World's Strongest Man Jon Pall Sigmarsson of Iceland. Recommended Equipment: 2 x Iso-Bows® available on Amazon or direct from Bullworker.com, strong rope and a towel.

TRISOmetrics™ - Advanced Science-Based High-Intensity Strength and Muscle Building.

This book has been approved by **TWiEA** – The World Isometric Exercise Association (www.TWiEA.com).

TRISOmetrics™ is an advanced, science-based high-intensity exercise system which combines 3 scientifically proven exercise techniques into a powerful new exercise system. TRISOmetrics™ can be performed with or without equipment, making it ideal for use at home or when travelling. It can also be used as part of a gym-based heavy exercise routine; the choice is yours. TRISOmetrics™ tells you which precisely type of exercise should be performed in specific sequence during a workout, how many repetitions, how long each exercise should be performed for, and how much rest time between exercises. It focusses on precision and quality in each exercise you perform combined with high-intensity to engage the maximum number of muscle fibres which keeps exercise sessions short, infrequent and highly effective. The system is ideal for people who don't confuse activity with accomplishment as most people seem to do when exercising. The TRISOmetric™ exercise system can also be performed with the Iso-Bow®, the Bullworker®, the Steel Bow®, the Bow Extension®, the Iso-Gym® or similar suspension trainers and with all gym-based exercise equipment.

The TRISO90™ Course – Advanced Strength and Muscle Building with The TRISOmetrics™ System.

This book has been approved by **TWiEA** – The World Isometric Exercise Association (www.TWiEA.com).

The TRISO90™ Course is a 534-page 90-day/12-week advanced bodybuilding and strength-building exercise course based on the TRISOmetrics™ exercise system. The TRISOmetric™ exercise system consists of three proven science-based exercise principles which when combined, form this highly advanced high-intensity exercise technique. The TRISO90™ Course progressively increases in difficulty over the 90-day/12-week period, with routines changed every two weeks to keep your muscles constantly challenged and responding to growth throughout the 90-day period. The TRISO90™ Course is ideal for people who already exercise regularly and want to take their workouts up to the next level. It is a pure strength and muscle building course making it ideal for the natural bodybuilder or for anyone who wants to get into the best shape possible in the minimum amount of time, with or without equipment.

The ISO90™ Course – The 12-Week/90-Day Shape-up and Get Strong Course.

This book has been approved by **TWiEA** – The World Isometric Exercise Association (www.TWiEA.com).

The ISO90™ Course is a comprehensive and complete step by step 90-day/12-week body shaping, bodybuilding and functional strength building course based on the ISOfitness™ system of isometric exercises. The ISO90™ course is ideal for beginners, advanced trainers alike. Your natural Adaptive Response™ mechanism means that whatever intensity you apply at whatever level you're at gives everyone roughly the same percentage of improvement. The ISO90™ course focusses the appliance of science in practical exercise and functional strength building. This makes the ISO90™ 90-day/12-week course, one of the fastest, and most efficient ways to get into shape, build muscle, and get strong. The ISO90™ course also allows you to benefit from a professional-level workout literally anywhere and on almost any location. Each week will build upon the gains made in previous weeks, with clear instruction and pictures to demonstrate how each exercise should be performed. Required Equipment: 2 x Iso-Bows® available on Amazon or from Bullworker.com

Workout at Work™ - Exercise at Work Without Anyone Even Knowing What You're Doing!

This book has been approved by **TWiEA** – The World Isometric Exercise Association (www.TWiEA.com).

Time is the #1 reason why people don't exercise. The average person spends over 10 years of their life at work over an average 45 year working life, which can mean sitting at a desk for 10-years! There is never enough time to spare in modern life and exercising the traditional way in a gym 3-days a week, will consume a further 4.27 years. A stark new warning from the Icahn School of Medicine at Mount Sinai School of Medicine in New York revealed that sitting at a desk working for more than 6 hours a day can cause potentially irreversible damage to your heart, increased levels of cholesterol, body fat, and insulin resistance which is a precursor to type 2 diabetes. What if you could exercise effectively while you were at work? What if a complete beginner could exercise with equal ease to an advanced athlete and all without leaving their desk? Now you can do exactly that with advanced isometric exercise. Amazingly research shows that even exercising 4 evenings a week after work, or for long periods over the weekend, won't fix the damage. However, if you performed just one simple 7-

second high-intensity exercise every 30 minutes while sitting at your desk, you'll gain maximum benefit from this scientifically proven system and at the end of a 9-hour working day, you will have performed a total-body 18-20 exercise routine. In exchange for as little as 126 seconds a day you'll feel better, become healthier, fitter, stronger, build more muscle and have more time to enjoy with your family and friends. Your boss won't complain either, because in exchange for just 126 seconds out of your working day, you'll be up to 30% more efficient at your job, and you'll take less time off sick. Required Equipment: 2 x Iso-Bows® available on Amazon or from Bullworker.com

Fitness on the Move™ - Enjoy Gym-Quality Workout Sessions ANYWHERE!

This book has been approved by **TWiEA** – The World Isometric Exercise Association (www.TWiEA.com).

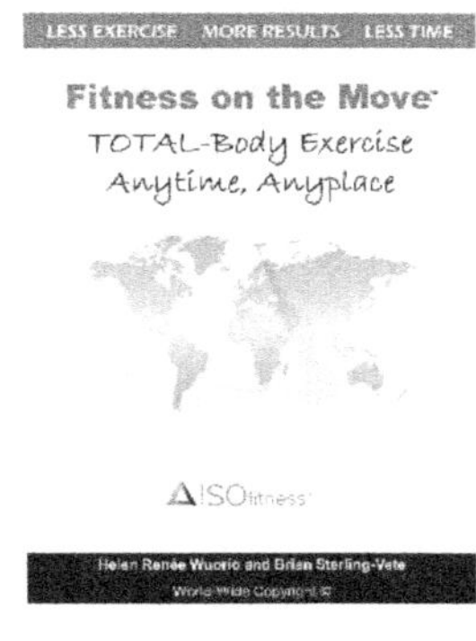

Being able to exercise anywhere is the key to getting the most from your workouts because you'll never be confined to a gym ever again. If you're travelling away from home for business or pleasure you can still maintain an optimised workout schedule to suit all levels of fitness from beginner right up to the advanced professional athlete. Advanced isometric exercise has been scientifically proven to be superior to traditional exercise methods in over 5,500 independent experiments. We've thoroughly tried and tested the Fitness on the Move™ system by performing full workout routines as passengers in cars, on trains, in cramped airline seats, on mountainsides, on beaches, and once even on the deck of a ship in a storm. The Fitness on the Move™ system allows a full-body workout in the smallest space humanly possible thanks to our Zero Footprint Workout™ concept. This means that if there is enough space to either sit down or stand upright, then you can perform a total-body exercise routine. Required Equipment: 2 x Iso-Bows® available on Amazon or from Bullworker.com

The Bullworker Bible™ The Ultimate Science-Based Guide to The Classic Personal Multi-Gym.

This book has been approved by **TWiEA** – The World Isometric Exercise Association (www.TWiEA.com).

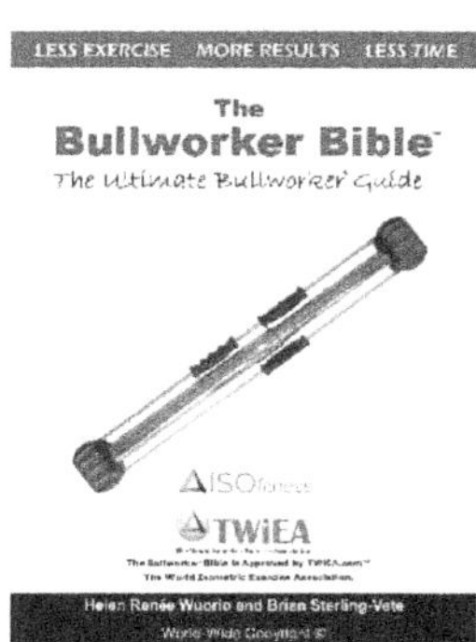

The Bullworker Bible™ is the definitive resource guide for all Bullworker® users, and it's the companion book for The Bullworker 90™ Course.

The Bullworker Bible™ is approved by the makers, and distributors of The Bullworker®, at Bullworker.com. It is the complete science-based user-friendly guide of how the Bullworker® should be used properly to deliver maximum results. It also shows you how to effectively use the Steel Bow®.

The Bullworker Bible™ gives you all the information that you always wanted to know, but the simple wall charts and basic instruction manuals didn't provide. It tells you about essential repetition-compression and speed control, correct breathing techniques, how Hooke's Law of physics applies to The Bullworker®, and about correct biomechanics to deliver the best results. The Bullworker Bible™ is also the essential guide for all users of the Bullworker X5, Bully Extreme, ISO 7x, and the Bullworker X7. Required Equipment: A Bullworker® Classic, or a similar device. Recommended Additional Equipment: Steel Bow®, Bow Extension® kit, 2 x Iso-Bows®, and the Bow Extension®.

The Bullworker 90™ Course – The Ultimate Science-Based 12-Week/90-Day Get strong and Grow Muscle Course Using the Classic Personal Multi-Gym.

This book has been approved by **TWiEA** – The World Isometric Exercise Association (www.TWiEA.com).

The Bullworker 90™ Course is the essential 90-day/12-week course for all Bullworker® users, and it's the companion book to The Bullworker Bible. Both books are approved by the makers of The Bullworker®.

The Bullworker 90™ is a 400+ page, science-based, user-friendly, step-by-step instruction course designed to increase strength, fitness, grow muscle, body-build, and increase power over a 90-day/12-week period. New exercises are added almost every week, with complete routine changes every two weeks.

Each week has a detailed note section, together with suggestions about exercise days, and rest times etc. This means that you know exactly what to do, and when to do it. The course includes step-by-step instruction, progressively increasing intensity over 90-days, isotonic/Isometric exercise combinations, and multi-angle isometric exercise combinations. The Bullworker 90™ Course can be used with the Bullworker® Classic, the Steel Bow®, the Bullworker X5, the Bully Extreme, the ISO 7x, and the Bullworker X7. The Bullworker 90™ Course also contains alternative/extra exercises using the Iso-Bow® and the Bow Extension® to increase the range and effectiveness of The Bullworker®. Required Equipment: A Bullworker® Classic, or a similar device. Recommended Equipment: Steel Bow®, Bow Extension® kit, 2 x Iso-Bows®.

The Bullworker Compendium™ - The Bullworker Bible™ and The Bullworker90™ Course Combined.

This book has been approved by **TWiEA** – The World Isometric Exercise Association (www.TWiEA.com).

At between 575 and 590 pages long, The Bullworker Compendium™ is the combination of both The Bullworker Bible™ and The Bullworker 90™ Course in a single huge book. To save printing costs the only thing we've eliminated are duplicated sections, everything else remains the same. This way we're able to offer both books in one for less than the combined price of the two other books. The Bullworker Compendium™ starts with The Bullworker Bible™, and at the end of that, it progresses seamlessly into The Bullworker 90™ Course.

The Doorway to Strength™ - Turn a Door into a Strength-Building Multigym.

This book has been approved by **TWiEA** – The World Isometric Exercise Association (www.TWiEA.com).

The Doorway to Strength™ shows how a simple door, doorway, and doorframe can be used to create a multi-gym of exercises using the amazing Iso-Bow® exerciser and the ISOfitness™ exercise system.

The Doorway to Strength™ demonstrates how to perform a host of powerful and effective exercises such as the door leg press and shoulder power push, together with many other exercises to work all the major body parts. The Iso-Bow® exerciser is probably the world's smallest and most powerful portable total-body exerciser.

The Iso-Bow® is so compact even that a pair of Iso-Bows® can easily fit into the pocket of an average pair of jeans.

However, even just one Iso-Bow® can deliver the perfect level of workout intensity for a beginner or an advanced athlete, and with no adjustment necessary.

The ISOfitness™ exercise system aims to deliver more results, in less time, and with less exercise than any other exercise system. Required Extra Equipment: 2 x Iso-Bows® (preferably 4), a solid door wedge/stop.

The Sixty Second ASS Workout™ - The Ultimate 60-Second Workout to Shape, Tone, Lift and Give You the Backside You've Always Wanted.

This book has been approved by **TWiEA** – The World Isometric Exercise Association (www.TWiEA.com).

The Sixty Second ASS Workout™, or SSASS™ workout, is the fastest and most effective "ass" workout ever devised. Based on the scientifically proven principles of advanced isometric exercise, the SSASS™ workout is a no-nonsense time-efficient workout that does everything you need to make your ass tight, firm, shapely and strong. The SSASS™ workout means no more time-wasting workouts where you twist, shake, wiggle around, kick your legs, or dance around for 30 minutes which might feel like fun but don't deliver the results you want. Everyone has 60 seconds of time to spare, even on the busiest day, so, you're just 60 seconds a day from having a great ass. Required Equipment: 2 x Iso-Bows available on Amazon or from Bullworker.com

Mental Martial Arts™ - intellectual Life and Business Combat Skills.

Brian Sterling-Vete's Mental Martial Arts is a system of intellectual life-combat skills which uses the tactics and principles of the physical martial arts. All interaction in life, in business, and when communicating with others is simply an exchange of energy, power and influence. Each party is always exerting maximum influence over the other as they attempt to gain the outcome they prefer over the weaker party. The more powerful and persuasive one will usually win unless the apparently 'weaker' person is trained in the Mental Martial Arts. Using this system you can learn to verbally, intellectually, and emotionally guide, channel and redirect the energy of others, even powerful people and large organisations. In doing so, you more frequently achieve the outcome that you desire in both life and business. It also contains a specific section about how to handle a potentially hostile media in the event of a crisis. In this section, Brian combines his system of Mental Martial Arts, together with the experience he gained in over a decade with BBC TV News, to help you and your organisation stay "Media Safe". www.mentalmartialarts.tv

Tuxedo Warriors™.

Tuxedo Warriors is the companion book to both The Tuxedo Warrior book and the movie. These books are the biography and autobiography of the iconic cult author, composer, moviemaker Cliff Twemlow. The original book ended at the beginning of what has been called by many 'the Golden Age' of Video Cinematography which Cliff Twemlow inspired. Tuxedo Warriors continues the story from the point when Cliff's original book finishes, and it is the most complete biography of Cliff Twemlow ever written. It's also the autobiography Brian Sterling-Vete who played a central role in this unique, entertaining and true story of two 'Renaissance-Men' and their adventures as guerrilla moviemakers. Amazingly, on their travels, they have documented encounters with witnesses of a poltergeist when living in Iceland, and a UFO encounter which several British Police officer also witnessed. Brian is probably the only person who can tell the most complete story about the life and adventures of Cliff Twemlow from the time it all began, right through until the end, with the sudden and untimely death of his close friend.

The Tuxedo Warrior™ by Cliff Twemlow – Prologue and epilogue by Brian Sterling-Vete.

There are many ways in which a Doorman can gain respect. Numerous methods applied to the principal. In my profession, every available technique must be utilised, depending on the situation and circumstances. Would-be transgressors either move-off the premises quietly acknowledging your diplomatic approach. Or, the other alternative whereby physical persuasion must be exercised, which either quells their pugilistic desires or it triggers their aggressive instincts, turning the whole incident into a bloody and violent encounter. 'The Tuxedo Warrior,' pulls no punches in its brawling, savage, colourful, and entertaining exposure of society's nightlife activities.

The above is the original text from the rear cover of Cliff's book. Cliff and I were extremely close friends, and I'm honoured to re-publish his original work, which completes the storyline of my own book, 'Tuxedo Warriors.' Where Cliff's original book finishes, 'Tuxedo Warriors' overlaps and begins to complete Cliff's colourful life story. I'm also honoured to be close friends with his eldest son, Barry Twemlow, and sincerely thank him for enabling this book and the others that Cliff wrote, to be re-published.

The Pike™ by Cliff Twemlow – Prologue and epilogue by Brian Sterling-Vete.

ITS FIRST VICTIMS - A screeching swan... A fisherman overboard... A drunken woman...

One by one, the mysterious killer in Lake Windermere claims its terrified victims. Tearing off limbs with its monstrous teeth, horribly mutilating bodies. Fear sweeps the peaceful holiday resort when experts identify the creature as a giant pike.... A hellish creature with the strength to rupture boats, and the anger to attack them. But for some, the terror becomes a bonanza—the traders who cater to the gathering crowds of ghouls on the shore. And, they will do anything to stop divers finding the creature. Meanwhile the ripples of bloodshed widen.... The Pike

The above is the original text from the rear cover of Cliff's book. I remember this book going into pre-production as a major movie in the early 1980s starring Joan Collins. Sadly, the financiers ran into personal difficulties and it was never made. Today, there is now renewed interest in this book as a screenplay and movie. In my own book 'Tuxedo Warriors' I tell the behind the scenes story of my close friend Cliff Twemlow, our adventures together as guerrilla moviemakers and The Pike.

The Beast of Kane™ by Cliff Twemlow – Prologue and epilogue by Brian Sterling-Vete.

When the Gordon Family open their door to a stray Elkhound, they unwittingly welcome-in the forces of evil. For, according to the local priest, the huge dog is Satan himself, fulfilling an ancient prophecy. But, no one will believe this warning... Even when sheep – and wolves – are mysteriously slaughtered. Even when frenzied pets turn on their owners. Even when Emily Forrest is savagely eaten alive – the first of many human victims. As winter tightens its icy grip on the remote town of Kane, its unprotected people must face an unearthly terror.

The above is the original text from the rear cover of Cliff's book. This was the first of Cliff's books to be accepted by Hammer Film Studios to be made into a big-screen horror movie, along with Cliff's other book, The Pike. More importantly, the reason why it was never to be made into a movie was no reflection on the book itself. It was entirely because of the increasing financial challenges Hammer Films were facing at that time. They were issues that were so serious, that they caused the unexpected and rapid decline of the studio.

Being American Married to a Brit™ - An Amusing Guide for Anglo-American Couples Divided by a Common Language and Culture.

When I first started dating my British man, I never gave a second thought about differences in language and culture. Why would I? After all, we Americans speak English, or do we...? As dating quickly turned into being engaged to and then getting married to my British gentleman, I also found that our common language and culture was a quirky, eye-opening, and highly amusing roller-coaster ride. At times during the most basic every-day conversations, I'd be listening to his words with glazed eyes, wondering what on earth he was saying. It really was as if we were both speaking a completely different language, even though the words that comprised the language were the same. I very quickly learned so much more about the language I was supposed to have been taught at school, the commonalities, the differences, and the good old-fashioned belly-laughs about it all that still punctuate our married life to this day. Since the Anglo-American royal marriage, these quirky anecdotes and fun-filled trivia topics have become more popular than ever. More importantly, I decided to write this book for, and dedicate it to all transatlantic couples who will regularly find themselves completely divided and confused by their common language and culture. www.MajorVision.com

Made in the USA
Monee, IL
23 November 2019